Marshal John Green-Volume 3

By: Daniel E. Henderson

Table of Contents:

Chapter:	Page:
1	2
2	37
3	59
4	87
5	120
6	146
7	180
8	210

Chapter 1

Marshal John Green vol. 3

Marshal John Green sat behind his desk as his wife Barbara, holding their new child, Ellie, walked into the jail with his and his three deputy's lunch. John beamed with pride when Barbara pulled the blanket back from the child's face and handed Ellie to her father.

He looked at his new child. "It's amazing how much she looks like you, honey. She's going to be a beautiful girl. I have a feeling we're going to be fighting off the boys when she gets older."

"That's going to be a while off. I want to see her stay safe in the meantime," Barbara said. " From what I understand, Tucson's a lot quieter than before you came and took office, but I still worry for her safety."

As John admired his daughter, shots came from outside the office. His new deputy, Billy Weems, lay on the boardwalk across the street from the office. John saw two horses galloping off, going east. As John ran over to help his deputy, Barbara came out of the office holding Ellie in her arms. The town's doctor happened to be in the saloon having a whisky, when he heard the shots. He ran out and reached the deputy as John crossed the street. He called out for a couple of men to help carry Billy to his office above the stables.

Two part-time deputies had just saddled their horses and come over to the jail. John got his horse from the stable, and the three rode off and followed the trail of the two men who had done the shooting. Although they were a half hour ahead, their trail wasn't hard to follow. They were surprised the men hadn't gone south to Nogales.

Early that evening, John, and his two deputies, caught up to the outlaws. They had made the mistake of thinking they had gotten a good enough start. Brett, one of the two deputies with the Marshal, spotted smoke from a campfire well off the trail. The three dismounted and quietly made their way to their quarries campsite. John got closer to listen to their conversation, before showing himself.

One of the men put his cup of coffee down. "Of all the people you could've shot, why did it have to be a deputy sheriff?"

"Being a little liquored up, I didn't pay much attention to that," the man said. "Being a deputy, I figure they'll have a posse out here first thing in the morning. We better clear out, as soon as it gets light."

After finishing his coffee, the other man said. "Don't know about you, but I don't think I'm going to get much sleep tonight. You know, if that deputy dies, we'll both hang."

"I don't think you have to worry about that if we get out early. We still have a couple days ride ahead of us to get to Las Cruces and another day to Albuquerque."

"If we see a posse, we might be smart to head south to El Paso and then into Mexico."

The Marshal heard enough. He and his two deputies slowly made their way to the campfire and got up to within twenty feet of the two men.

John said. "Keep your hands away from your guns, and slowly put your hands up."

One of the outlaws said, "I understand the man we shot was a deputy. He cheated us in a card game and ran out the door of the saloon."

"That's a lie," John said. "Billy Weems never drank, smoked, or gambled. You'll have to come up with a better one than that, and pray he's still alive. I'm not going to tell you again, put your hands in the air.

Knowing they didn't have a chance, the two men complied. The two deputies with the Marshal went to the men at the fire and disarmed them both. Being dark, the ride back to

Tucson would be treacherous. They tied the men to a nearby tree in a sitting position, and pulled out their own bedrolls. The Marshal and his two deputies enjoyed the hot coffee and grub at the campfire before turning in.

Early the next morning, one of John's deputies fixed coffee, hardtack, and biscuits they had brought with them. After breakfast, the two men, after relieving themselves in the bushes, were tied to their horses, and the five rode southwest, toward Tucson.

They got to Tucson late in the afternoon, tired and hungry. John put the two men in a cell while Brett and Fred took their horses and the Marshal's to the stable. John went directly up to the doctor's office above the stable.

"Well, Doc, how's Billy doing?"

"I almost lost him last night, but he's still hanging on. Did you get those two?"

"You know, Doc, that's a silly question. I wouldn't come back without them, dead or alive. They had the good sense to give up."

"Did they tell you why they had to shoot him?"

"They claimed he cheated them at poker," John said. "Had it been anybody else, maybe, but not Billy."

"The only time I ever saw Billy in that saloon was on official business for you. I think he's awake in the other room if you want to talk to him."

The Marshal walked into the bedroom where Billy lay. He slept as John walked over and pulled up a chair. Ten minutes later Billy awoke. He looked over at John and smiled.

"We got the two guys. You have any idea why they shot you?" John said.

"That's probably because I tried to arrest them for holding up the general store and beating up Hank. I probably should've just shot them."

"Doc told me he got hold of Margaret to let her know what happened to you. She's been in here since he called her, and just left to get a bite of lunch."

"With my arm like it is, I doubt I'm going to be able to do you much good, at least for a while." Billy said. "Doc told me I almost bought it last night."

"Brett and Sam have both offered to fill in for you until you get back," John said. "I may just go ahead and hire them both. I've been thinking about putting them on full-time, anyway."

"You're not getting any argument out of me," Billy said. "They're both good guys and I really think we can use them."

"Well, I guess I better get back to Barbara and the kid."

"Hey, congratulations, Doc told me you had a new daughter," Billy said. "For her sake, I sure hope she takes after her mother."

John laughed at that and left the room. He went over and joined Doc for a cup of coffee at his table.

"How long do you think he's going to be tied up?" John said. "He seems to be in good spirits. I know one of those shots got his arm. What about the other one?"

"It was a chest wound and, like I said, I almost lost him last night. Luckily the bullet just broke a couple ribs, and I was able to pull it out, and clean it up."

"Sounds like he was lucky," John said. "I imagine those two in my jail are going to be happy to hear about that."

"Maybe you ought to hold off on telling them for now," Doc said. "I'm sure Billy's going to be okay, but just let them stew a while."

The Marshal shook his head, and left the Doc's office. He went back to his office to make sure Brett could handle things and check on the prisoners before heading home.

Barbara waited at the door when he rode up. He put his horse in the barn after giving him a good brushing, a bag of oats and an apple off their tree. He walked up the stairs and kissed his wife. With his arm around her, the two went into the house. He could hear Ellie screaming her head off in the bedroom. He couldn't wait to hold her, as well. He went into the bedroom and picked up his daughter, just what she needed to quiet down. Barbara came in and sat down in the rocking chair. John handed their daughter to her. He enjoyed watching his wife as she nursed Ellie.

The marshal went outside to the pump, cleaned up, and shaved to get ready for dinner. He walked back into the house and went into the bedroom, undressed, and lay down on the large feather bed, definitely an improvement over a bedroll on the rocky ground. He fell asleep as soon as his head hit the pillow. Barbara came in from the other bedroom shortly, and lay next to her husband. She felt like the luckiest woman in the world, although she constantly feared for her husband's safety.

The next morning, Barbara got up when she heard Ellie getting restless, and went in and fed her. She then went to the kitchen to fix a breakfast of coffee, toast, bacon and eggs for her husband. John awoke to the smell coming from the kitchen. He got dressed and joined his wife at the table.

"If that tastes anything like it smells, I think I may be in heaven," John said. "Sure beats hardtack and coffee, even with biscuits."

"I have homemade biscuits with jelly from our guava tree," Barbara said. "I hope it tastes good."

"I won't have any complaints. You know it's my favorite."

After breakfast, and giving his wife a lasting kiss and hug, John went out to the barn and saddled up. He noticed it looked like another hot day as he rode toward town, and his office. The remainder of a dust storm continued to blow in his face as he reached town. Leaving his horse at the livery stable, the marshal went to his office. Sam sat behind the small desk next to John's.

"I see you slept in a little this morning," Sam said. "Brett's across the street at the saloon. Cecil Sutton came over and told us there was a ruckus down there."

John walked across the room and pulled his gun and holster off the hook on the wall. "I guess I better go over there and be sure everything's okay."

Sam promised to hold down the fort until the Marshal got back. John walked out the door and over to the saloon. He heard yelling, and a gunshot. He walked in through the batwing doors, and saw Brett holding a gun, and a man on the floor.

The Marshal walked into the saloon. "Okay Brett, what's going on in here?"

"Our friend here began running his mouth off. The bartender told him to stop, and the guy pulled a gun on him. His first shot missed, I don't know if that was by accident. I wasn't about to take a chance."

"Okay Lee, what's your side of all this," John said, looking down at the floor.

"The barkeep started it, and I finished it, that's all."

John turned his attention to the bartender. "What happened, Zeke? Did you liquor him up too much?"

The bartender looked at John. "I kept telling him to stop bothering other customers. These two gents just got here from Tombstone, and they were both dry. Lee here kept trying to start a fight with them for some reason."

Brett helped Lee to his feet. John could tell by the way he staggered, that Lee wasn't on the up and up. He told Brett to take him to jail to sober up. John again looked over at Zeke.

"Zeke, I told you before, when these guys start getting drunk, not to give them anymore."

"Look marshal, when a guy points a gun at you, you tend to do what he says. My chandelier got hit. Who's going to pay for that?"

"I'll talk to Lee. He hasn't got any money but, maybe he can do some work around here to pay for it."

The Marshal walked over to his office where Brett sat on the front porch with his feet up on the hitching-rail. John nodded, went into his office and sat down. He began going through some of the wanted posters brought in by stage that morning. He took them outside and handed them to Brett to go through. Brett had an amazing memory for faces and after looking at them, took them over to the saloon and showed them around. Most of the outlaws had hefty rewards on their heads. Some were marked "dead or alive". Afterward he returned to his chair outside the office. The rest of the day stayed reasonably quiet.

John left the office early and went back to his farm. He got the buggy out of the barn and cleaned it up and got it ready for church the next day. After cleaning up, he went inside the farm house and spent a quiet evening with his wife and daughter.

The next morning Barbara got up early to get Ellie ready for the church service. The baby would be christened that morning, and Barbara dressed her in a beautiful christening gown, with a red bow on the front, she had made. She then went into the kitchen and fixed coffee and a nice breakfast and put it on the table. John came out dressed in a handsome black suit and string tie. The two enjoyed a lingering kiss, sat down, said grace, and had breakfast. Barbara cleaned up the kitchen, went to the bedroom and got dressed. They got on the buggy and left for the church.

As they arrived in front of the church, John went around and helped his wife and daughter off the vehicle. Several church members, just getting there, went over to see John and Barbara's new daughter. The minister came down the wooden steps of the church and over to the buggy. He smiled favorably at the couple's daughter. Church bells rang out, and everybody went into the church and sat down. Barbara looked up at the ceiling and admired the beautiful architecture. Angels painted on the ceiling showed hours of work. John and Barbara brought Ellie up to the front of the church where the minister blessed the child, and started flinging water at the child's face with his fingers. Ellie began showing off her lungs to the whole congregation, as the audience laughed.

After the service, the church members came over to John and Barbara and congratulated them. By this time Ellie had calmed down and the people of the congregation admired her. Many of the women asked to hold her. Later, John and Barbara took their daughter out to the buggy and headed home.

Barbara fixed up a picnic basket, while John gave the horse oats and water. The three got onto the buggy, and went to a nearby Glenn, covered with trees and Lake Tanganyika. The green grass had a fresh smell to it as John laid out a blanket. After a memorable afternoon, the family went back to their farm. Barbara nursed Ellie, put her to bed and joined her husband in front of a fire.

The Marshal got back to the office the next morning. Jack, another of John's deputies sat at the desk.

John walked over to the deputy. "Everything stay quiet yesterday, Jack?"

"Oh, one of the girls working upstairs in the saloon got beat up by one of her customers. He was lying on the floor when I got there. He's in the jail now."

"What happened to him?"

"Some of the men didn't take too kindly to seeing a woman treated that way," Jack said. "A couple of the guys heard her scream and went upstairs to her room. They pulled the guy out and threw him down the stairs."

"Sounds like the guy had been drinking, or on opium?" John said, as he walked back to the cells.

The marshal saw the prisoner, who looked pretty banged up, badly bruised and barely able to move. The Marshal went out and told Jack to go down and get the doc. A few minutes later the two came back. Doc went back to the cell to examine the man. He removed the man's shirt and felt his chest.

"John, the guy's got a few broken ribs, and possibly a broken arm. His legs seem to be okay," Doc said. "Better get a couple guys to bring him over to my office. He' in pretty bad shape, and will be for a few days. You can bring him back here after that, if you want."

"I think he's probably learned his lesson. He may have to patronize a different saloon in another part of town so those guys at Zeke's can't get to him."

The Marshal got two of his deputies to take the man to the doctor's office above the stable. The guy moaned a lot during the transport, and several of the men on the street started shouting obscenities at the guy.

A man pictured on one of the wanted posters had gone into the saloon. Zeke quietly asked one of the men sitting at the bar to go get the Marshal. The man crossed the street and came down to the Marshal's office.

"Marshal, Zeke sent me down here," the man said. "One of those guys on the wanted posters is in the saloon. He looks kind of mean."

"Frank, you stay here. Brett, go get a couple deputies and meet me at the saloon. Don't go in until I get there."

"Will do, Marshal, the deputies were in here a bit ago after taking the guy down to doc." Jack said. "They told me they were heading down to the bank."

The Marshal pulled the forty-five Smith & Wesson off-the-wall and went to the saloon. He had no intention of getting in a one-on-one fight inside. He waited for his three deputies and then went into action. One of the deputies waited outside while Brett and John went in. John saw his quarry sitting alone at a table with his back to the wall. Brett put on the act of being drunk.

"Who the hell do you think you are?" Brett said to the barkeep in a loud voice hoping to distract the man. "Give me a bottle of whiskey, and don't give me no trouble about it."

The other deputy noisily made his way through the batwing doors of the saloon. Before anybody in the bar knew what happened, John had the forty-five pointed at the outlaw's forehead. Brett came over and disarmed the man and pulled him to his feet. The two law men handcuffed and ushered the man out of the saloon and over to the jail.

"What the hell do you guys think you're doing?" Gerald said. "I haven't done anything."

"You're under arrest for bank robbery, and the murder of a clerk and Deputy Marshal in Phoenix," John said. "My deputies will accompany you on the next stage going there. I would advise you not to say anything."

After the busy morning, John welcomed the sight of his wife and daughter, who had brought down lunch for him and the deputies. The four men sat in the office telling stories about the morning's activities. John tried, unsuccessfully, to get them to ease up in front of his wife. About that time, Loren, from the cafe brought in lunch for the new inmate and took it back to his cell. John warned Loren to just set it on the floor and get out of there, which he did.

"That's one mean-looking bastard you have back there, Marshal," the young man said. "I recognize him from the wanted posters you guys put up."

Loren left the office and headed back to the café down the street.

John took Ellie from Barbara and began to rock her in his arms. She looked at her father, smiled at him, which melted his heart. Between that and the remarks his deputies were making, for the first time he began to realize what would happen to his wife and daughter if anything were to happen to him. He handed Ellie back to his wife, got off his chair, accompanied them out to the buggy, and kissed the two of them goodbye.

John watched as she left and continued watching her and his daughter through the window as she turned the buggy around and left for home. He then turned his attention to the paperwork he had on his desk. It would have to be finished before the stage came in the next morning. After completing it, he walked back to the cell to check on his prisoner.

"Marshal, can't you just hang me here and get it over with?" The man said. "I've had enough living and it would be easier on both of us."

"It probably would, but you know I can't," John said. "It's hard for me to feel sorry for you. I understand the people you murdered in Phoenix had families. They want to see you hang and, frankly, I can't blame them."

The Marshal started back out to the office when he heard the door open. Brett brought in a man who got drunk and started a fight in the saloon. John often wondered what possessed some men to act this way. He didn't recognize the man, and figured he didn't live in Tucson.

"Who do you have there, Brett?"

"This guy got liquored up and started a fight over at Jake's," the Marshal said. "He's with a cattle drive from Dallas, heading out to Los Angeles, California."

Brett took the prisoner back to the jail cells, leaving an empty cell between his prisoner and the outlaw. The man fell asleep as soon as he hit the bunk. He noticed the outlaw slept on the cot with his back to the red-brick wall. Brett went out and sat down across from the Marshal.

"I think we're going to have more trouble tonight," Brett said. "Those cowhands have had a long hard ride."

"I think you better go out to their campsite and have a talk with the crew boss," the Marshal said. "Better check at the saloon to be sure he's not there."

"Good idea, I'll get going now. The other two deputies can handle any other problems."

After Brett left, the Marshal went outside to get a little air. He sat on the bench and put his feet up on the hitching rail. He fell into a light sleep until another shooting in front of the saloon woke him. John got to his feet and arrived there shortly after one of his deputies. The other deputy arrived minutes later.

"Stay out of this, marshal," the man said, addressing one of the deputies.

With his gun pointed at the man the Marshal said, "Put the gun down, and I mean right now!"

The man turned slightly, and saw the marshal meant business. He slowly lowered his weapon, handing it to the deputy. Standing in front of the saloon, John figured both had been drinking. He took the man to the jail, while the two deputies picked up the victim and took him to the doc's office where he later died.

John went into the saloon and walked over to Jake. He sat down on a barstool and ordered a beer.

"Okay Zeke, do you have any idea what that was all about?"

"Two of them started a fight. I told them to get the hell out of here. They went outside and, the first thing I knew, I heard a gunshot. I got "Old Betsy", Zeke said, pointing to his rifle. I headed to the door, when I heard you guys out there."

"You know what they were fighting about?"

"Kind of; the guy that was shot said something about the other man's wife, but that's about all I heard."

"Sounds like a good way to start a fight. Do you know if they were part of the cattle drive here from Texas?"

"I'm pretty sure they were. I didn't recognize them. They came in a little after some of the others from the drive had left."

"Well, I sent Brett out to have a talk with the drive-boss. I'm hoping he can straighten out his men. If not, I told Brett to tell him not to let any of his men come back to town."

"I can understand that," Jake said. "I hope it doesn't come to that."

John finished his beer and went back to the office. He walked back to check on his prisoners. The four stayed quiet. The marshal returned to his office and sat behind his desk. About that time, Sam came in to relieve him.

"I understand we're having a little trouble with the cowhands," Sam said. "I met Brett out on the trail, he'll be here shortly. He told me he had a talk with the crew boss, and the two had an understanding. Why don't you go home, we can handle anything that comes up."

"I might just do that. I'll see you in the morning. Thanks Sam."

Walking down toward the stable, John met Brett coming towards the Jail.

"Sam said you and the cattle boss came to an agreement. Is everything okay?"

"Yeah, he said he'd have a talk with the guys and let them know if they caused any trouble none of them could come back into town."

"That's good. Thanks Brett. I'll see you in the morning."

The Marshal continued down to the stable, got his horse saddled, and headed home. After getting his horse settled in, he went to the house. Barbara stood on the porch waiting for him. He cleaned up and walked to the steps and put his arm around his wife's waist, and the two went into the large room. Ellie slept in her room. Barbara had fixed a dinner of steak, potatoes, warm bread, and to top it off, coffee and apple pie. After cleaning up in the kitchen, Barbara came into the living room. John put his arm around her when she sat next to him on the couch.

The weather had turned cold that night and they enjoyed a warm fire and conversation. John went down the hall to see his daughter before turning in for the night. Barbara followed and, after nursing the child, joined John in the feather bed. The two made love that night before falling asleep.

The next morning, they awoke early, and spent a little time cuddling. Afterward, Barbara got up and went to the kitchen to put on coffee, and fixed breakfast for her and her husband. As he finished his coffee, Barbara went into the other bedroom to get their daughter. She started nursing the child as John left for work.

John rode into town in the cold weather. The marshal stabled his horse and walked down to the office. Sam slept behind the desk when John walked in. Slamming the door woke him up.

"Good morning, John, I was just grabbing a quick nap. I had a busy night, and we have three more men in the jail cells. If this keeps up we may have to have more cells built."

"So, what happened?" John said. "Were they involved in the same thing?"

"Two of them were. Claude Martin came out of the saloon, drunk, and started making a pest of himself with two women," Sam said. "The other two tried to hold up the Assay Office shortly after closing, bad mistake. Pete got the drop on them as they walked through the door. They dropped their guns when they saw his rifle. He had his assistant come get me."

"Do you know these two?" John said.

"I've seen them around. They told me they're from the other side of Tucson. I figured you'd want to talk to them."

The Marshal walked back to the cell holding Claude Martin.

"Well Claude, I understand you got yourself into a little trouble last night," the Marshal said. "What was it all about?"

"I just accidentally rubbed up against those women. "You've got to believe me, Marshal."

"I don't. I have a feeling Nancy's not going to believe you either. I told you before not to get drunk in that saloon. Buy a bottle and take it home if you want."

"You know Nancy's a teetotaler," Claude said. "She'd never let me bring a bottle into the house."

John opened the cell door. "Go on home, Claude. "The next time you're in here you're going to stay for ten days."

Claude got out of there in a hurry. John walked down to the cell holding the men that tried to hold up the Assay Office. They got up and came to the cell door.

"Don't waste your breath," John said. "The folks in this town don't take kindly to people who try to steal from them."

The two men looked at each other, and returned to their cots. John went to the cell holding the man charged with murder. He sat up on the edge of the bunk when he heard the Marshal talking to the others.

The Marshal turned his attention to the prisoner in the other cell. "The stage is down at the livery stable. Get your stuff and come over to the door."

The Marshal handcuffed the man through the cell door, and opened it, ordering him to come out. Sam handed John the paperwork on the prisoner as the two walked by the desk, and out the door. The Marshal took the prisoner to the stage and put him inside. Two deputies boarded as well.

"Say hi to Marshal Matt when you get to Phoenix," John said. "Be sure to let him know this guy is extremely dangerous, and nobody to play around with."

"Will do Marshal, we'll catch the return stage in the morning."

The Marshal slapped the side of the coach after closing the door. The driver brought the horses to life. The stage took off down the street in a cloud of dust. John went back into his office. The other two prisoners would be leaving Phoenix the morning after the circuit judge came to town in a couple of days for their trial. Barbara came in with lunch for John and Sam, who stayed on to fill in for one of the deputies taking the prisoner to Phoenix.

"Where's my girl?" John said, as Barbara set their lunch down.

"Oh, I had her tied to the back of the horse. I think she fell off on the way." Barbara said, with a grin. "She's at the general store. Millie insisted I leave her there until I got ready to leave for home."

Later that afternoon, a rider came into town at full gallop on a horse he got at a nearby farm. He ran into the marshal's office out of breath with a bloody head.

"Marshal, the stage was stopped about thirty miles out of town. Three masked men shot the driver and two deputies. They took the passenger, sitting next to me, and escaped. One of the men knocked me out with the butt of his gun. I guess he thought I was dead. I took one of the deputy's horses, and came back here as fast as I could."

The marshal took deputies, Sam and Brett, and headed out. An hour later they came upon the stage. A couple of men were there rustling around with the strong box when the deputies arrived. John arrested both of them and had Sam take them and the empty strongbox back to Tucson. The outlaws' trail became a little hard to follow until they split up. Although John wanted to be on the trail of the two escapees, he wasn't sure which would be the right one. He sent Brett in a northerly direction toward Phoenix. He followed the other two outlaws heading west, toward the mountains between Arizona and California. Sand blowing in his face made the ride almost unbearable; he figured the outlaws would have the same problem.

Late that evening John came upon the campsite of the two he followed. He made his way behind a few trees until he got within shouting distance of the men. He could tell they were not the escapees, but figured they were the two that rescued them. He waited a few minutes until both had coffee in their hands before showing himself.

He slowly made his way to the campfire, with both guns drawn. The two men realized the marshal had the drop on them.

"Slowly put your hands in the air, and don't think about getting cute," John said. "I want you to very easily, with two fingers, take your guns out of the holsters and throw them over here."

"What do you want with us Marshal?" One of the men said. "We haven't done anything."

"Ringo and Charlie?" John said. "I haven't seen you two in a while. Last time I put you in jail, the judge gave you ten years. How come you're out?"

"We did six years. We were let out on good behavior."

"Good behavior?" John said. "That's a laugh—Uh, Uh, you'll never make it to your guns, so don't even try it. Stand up, put your hands behind your back, and walk over to those trees. I want you to get on your knees on each side of that large one."

John carefully made his way over to the men, ordering them not to try anything. He had them handcuff each other around the tree trunk. Being a little late, John decided to make camp. He wondered how Brett had faired with the two escapees. He took out his horse blanket and sleeping bag and got as comfortable as he could. The wind had died down a bit, but the weather remained cold. He felt bad leaving the two handcuffed to the tree, but self-preservation kicked in.

Early the next morning, John awoke and fixed coffee. He doubted his prisoners got much sleep. He took one of the handcuffs off, letting the two get up and go out to the tumbleweeds. After relieving themselves, the two stumbled back to the campfire, where John poured them each a cup of coffee and pulled some hardtack out of their saddlebags.

The marshal tied the two men to their horses, handcuffing them to the saddle horns. They headed out southeast to return to Tucson. John worried about Brett, but figured he'd better worry about getting his prisoners back before doing anything.

Brett had not returned when John got back. He took his two prisoners into the jail and put the men in cells.

"Is Brett with you?" Sam said.

"No, I was hoping he'd be here when I got back. I'm going to go out there and find him," John said. "I need to run by the farm to let Barbara know what's going on."

John rode back to the farm, took the horse into the barn, rubbed him down, and gave him a bucket of oats. He went in the house to talk to Barbara. After a quick cup of coffee and a sandwich, John went back out to the barn, got the other horse saddled, and rode off toward Phoenix.

The marshal took the stagecoach trail between Phoenix and Tucson, figuring that would be Brett's most likely route. Again the wind blew hard and sand made the trip miserable, but thankfully it calmed down. About an hour later, John saw dust up ahead. He breathed a sigh of relief as he saw two riders get closer to him, a third strapped over his saddle. John turned around and waited until his deputy got there.

"I take it he tried to make trouble," John said, looking at the guy lying across the saddle.

"Yeah, he did," Brett said. "He drew a gun on me even though I had mine pointed straight at him. I guess he just didn't want to go back to prison."

"Well, I'm glad you're okay. I've got my guys back in jail."

The three made their way to Tucson. After securing their prisoner in jail, John took the dead man to the undertaker before taking the horses back to the stable, while Brett put the outlaw in jail and took the guns into the office.

Brett went up the street for a beer at the saloon. The marshal came from the stable to the office, and then over to the saloon for a beer as well. John deputized one of his friends, and had him go over to the office, and take over for Sam. Afterwards all three lawmen headed for home.

The marshal rode back to the farmhouse, took the horse into the barn, and gave him a good rubdown and a bucket of oats. He pulled a couple apples off the tree outside and gave both horses a treat and after cleaning up went into the house where Barbara had dinner waiting. She put her arms around her husband when he came in the door. John could hear Ellie in the back room clapping her hands and playing. Before dinner, John walked back and picked her up. Sometimes he tended to forget how much he loved his two girls.

The next morning the Marshal got up and out early not waking his wife. The weather still cold had John in his overcoat. He rode in and left his horse at the livery stable. He walked into the office and to his desk. The man he deputized the evening before sat in front of the prisoners in the jail cell.

"Good morning, marshal," Bob said. "You look better than you did last night. I thought you'd be in a little later this morning."

"I could've stayed in that bed all day," John said. "The circuit judge is coming this morning and we have to get these guys ready for court. The paperwork is on my desk."

John walked across the street, got coffee for him and his deputy, and returned to the office. The circuit judge showed up that morning on the early stage. John and Bob handcuffed the three prisoners and took them by buckboard to the county courthouse down the street. A light rain began to fall as they reached the courthouse.

After taking them up the steps of the courthouse, John released the three into the custody of their attorneys. The men were taken down the hall to get cleaned up. They were well guarded by deputies.

The three were taken into the courtroom where they sat next to the attorneys. John sent Bob back over to watch the jail until Sam showed up. One of the deputies called the room to order. The jury and onlookers were seated and the judge entered the courtroom. The two amateur bank robbers were both found guilty and sentenced to five years in prison. Gerald, the next man called, went to the front of the courtroom.

One of the court's deputies said, "Gerald Marston, you are charged with first-degree murder and robbery. How do you plea?"

Seeing John in the courtroom, along with two witnesses, he decided on a guilty plea, hoping the judge would grant leniency. The judge saw through that, and sentenced him to the gallows the next morning. The other two were both given harsh sentences in their attempt to free Marston. The three were taken down the hall where they surrendered their property. The two men were taken back to the jail, where they would later be transported to the Yuma territorial prison.

The next morning the light rain picked up as deputies took Gerald Marston to the gallows at an area behind the jail. Several people, including the marshal and Bob, looked on as a minister waited at the top of the stairs, and a deputy led the defendant to the noose. The process ended in minutes and the corpse taken to the undertaker for burial.

John never got pleasure from witnessing executions. Members of the family of the men Gerald had killed came to John and thanked him. He expressed his condolences to those people and returned to the jail. He sat at his desk when Bob and Brett returned to the office.

Barbara came into the office a little later and handed Ellie to John while she fixed lunch for the men.

"You got out a little early this morning," Barbara said. "I remembered you had the court date this morning, so I fixed you something a little special for lunch today."

"Fried chicken and potato salad," Brett said. "You need to have these court appearances a little more often John!"

Bob looked over at Brett, "you can say that again."

The lunch came in for the prisoners a few minutes later. Cecil took it back to the cells knowing it would probably be their last decent meal for some time to come. He came back out a little later, acknowledged Barbara and Ellie, and headed back to the café.

Knowing John needed rest, Sam said, "You know John, Bob and I can easily handle anything that comes in. If we need you I can always ride out to your place to get you. You and Brett had a rough couple of days, so why don't you call it a day and go on home."

Barbara looked at John in total agreement. John nodded his head in an affirmative gesture and followed Barbara and his daughter out the door. After helping them onto the buggy, John walked down to the stable and picked up his horse. The stable hands had already given the animal water and oats.

John stopped at the saloon for a beer before returning home. That turned out to be a bit of a mistake. A bar fight turned deadly as John walked in. The man turned his gun on the marshal, and shot John in his left shoulder. Being right-handed, John shot and killed the man before putting pressure on his own wound. Zeke ran out from behind the bar and over to the marshal.

Deputies Bob, Sam, and Brett ran to the saloon when they heard the gunshots. Seeing his boss with a bloodied shirt, Brett immediately helped him over to a table. After seeing what happened, Sam sent Bob to get the undertaker and then talked to the bartender. "What happened here, Zeke?"

"It all happened so fast," Zeke said. "I don't think either man had that much to drink, but they were gambling. I heard the man who shot the marshal, say something about being cheated by the man he shot. That's when the marshal came in. I think if the guy recognized him, he would've surrendered peacefully."

The marshal stepped forward. "Do you know either of these men?"

"They've both been in here for the last couple of days," Zeke said. "This is the first time I noticed any trouble between them. One of them told me he was up here from Texas on a cattle drive."

Since neither of these men had been drinking, the marshal decided against putting a stop to the men on the cattle drive coming in. The undertaker got a couple of the men in the saloon to carry the two men to his office. John had a beer, and headed over to the doctor's office and had the bullet that grazed his shoulder, taken out.

The marshal got back to his farm, put the horse up, and went into the house. Barbara lay in the back room feeding Ellie. John could never get enough of watching the two of them. He went outside to the pump to clean up while Barbara put dinner on the table for them.

"What happened? —you've been wounded," Barbara said.

"I walked in on a gunfight. The guy was rattled, and took a shot at me. I'll be all right in a day or two."

"I worry about this sort of thing all the time."

"I know, honey, but it comes with the job," John said. "Something smells awfully good in here."

John sat down at the table to a dinner of pot roast and potatoes, one of his favorite meals. Barbara brought over a hunk of apple pie, and coffee, when he finished.

After dinner, she cleaned things up, went into the other room, and sat on the couch next to her husband. John put his arm around her, and pulled her to him. They walked to the bedroom, and checked on Ellie on the way.

The next morning Barbara changed the bandage on John's shoulder before he left for town. Brett came out to the porch.

"Marshal, there's been trouble up in Tombstone," Brett said. "Dan Dixon was shot and killed during a bank robbery up there early this morning. Ronnie followed them down here to the Pioneer hotel.

"Dan? Oh damn. Come on, let's go," the marshal said, pulling his gun belt off the hook.

The two law-men rode to the hotel. Frankie, the hotel owner welcomed John and Brett when they walked in.

"Hello, Marshal, what brings you down here?"

"I understand you checked a couple of guys in this morning?" John said. "I need to talk to them."

"Yeah, they're upstairs in room fifteen. Did they do something?"

"I don't know yet. Don't let anybody go up there until I come back down here."

Frankie gave the marshal an affirmative headshake, "Will do, marshal."

The marshal and Brett made their way up the stairway with their guns drawn. When they got to the room, they stood on either side of the door. John reached over and knocked.

"This is U.S. Marshal John Green, open up."

Chapter 2

A hail of gunfire came through the door about twenty seconds later. John counted the number of shots fired before kicking the door in. Both men stood by the bed, their guns clicked as they attempted another shot. Brett took a shot at Kansas City Lou, hitting him in the heart. Minnesota Max dropped his gun and put his hands over his head. The marshal put the man in cuffs, while Brett picked up his victim and carried him out to the front to be picked up by the undertaker.

Another of John's deputies arrived and took the prisoner back to the office and threw him in a cell. John and Brett rode back to the office.

"Brett, get Pete in here. I have a job for him," John said. "I think I saw him outside this morning."

A few minutes later Brett and Pete walked into the office.

"Good morning Pete. You're my only single deputy. I have a temporary duty for you. You may even want to make it permanent. Dan Dixon was shot and killed in an early-morning bank robbery. He had just taken over for Wyatt Earp. I need you to go up there and run the office until we can find somebody for the job."

"I'll get right up there, Marshal," I haven't got anything holding me here, so I may just take you up on that. It's too bad about Dan. He was a good guy."

Pete handed John his deputy sheriff's badge, took a marshal's badge, and left the office. John went in to have a talk with his prisoner.

"Okay, Mitch, what happened up in Tombstone this morning?"

"We didn't intend to kill anybody, Marshal. We busted open the door to the bank when the marshal came in. We ducked behind the counter and Gary shot him."

"Gary, huh, what happened? Did he get a little trigger-happy?"

"We just got out of jail in Phoenix. Neither of us wanted anything to do with another prison sentence."

"Well, I can guarantee you don't have to worry about that. Dan Dixon was a good guy and a good friend."

Mitch knew exactly what John meant when he said that. Bank robbery is one thing, but murder is a hanging offense. He sat back on the cot, putting his head in his hands. John went back out to his desk. Brett had left to go out and patrol the streets. John walked out and sat on the bench in front of the jail, putting his feet up on the hitching rail. The weather had turned decent. He lifted his left arm and waved to Pete as he rode by.

John thought about the earlier days when he and Dan had first come here. Dan worked under him as a deputy for about a year before taking on the job in Tombstone. Married, with two kids, both he and his wife enjoyed living in Tombstone.

The marshal saw Barbara and Ellie coming down the street in the buggy. Brett and Sam both came back to the office when they saw her. Les came in shortly after.

"How's the arm, honey?" Barbara said. "I hope you've been able to take it easy this morning."

John smiled at her, got off the bench, walked over to the buggy and picked up his daughter. Brett came over and helped Barbara down. She brought the lunch basket in and laid out meals for the four men. A few minutes later, Loren came in with the lunch for both Mitch, and a couple of other prisoners, and left minutes later.

Barbara had made up roast beef sandwiches, and her famous potato salad. Brett poured coffee for Barbara and the three deputies. The four men thoroughly enjoyed their lunch. Ellie sat on her father's lap, and he gave her little bites of his lunch. Barbara scolded him for that, but knew it wasn't going to harm the baby. After lunch John carried Ellie out to the buggy and helped Barbara onto the seat, after giving her a goodbye kiss.

After Barbara left, the deputies left the office to do their rounds. John went back into the office to do reports on the prisoners.

"The circuit judge will be coming here in the morning," Brett said.

John went back to the jail cell where Mitch lay down on the cot. In a way he felt sorry for the man, but he had no way of being sure which of the two bank robbers killed Dan Dixon. The other two prisoners were in there for drunk and disorderly, resulting in a young child possibly being crippled for life due to accidentally hitting the child during their fight.

After filling out the forms and getting them ready for the judge the next day, the marshal decided to leave a little early, when Sam came back. He went to the livery stable, picked up his horse, and headed for home. He got back, stabled the horse, got cleaned up and went inside. Barbara busied herself cleaning up the place and just finished as John came in. She went over and the two enjoyed a warm kiss.

"You look a little down tonight, Honey," Barbara said. "Is there anything wrong?"

"I guess I shouldn't be concerned. Mitch swears it was his partner that killed Dan Dixon. I think he's on the level but, on the other hand, that's not going to fly with the judge. I just hate to see somebody so young, hang."

"Come on, honey, this isn't the first time I've heard you say something like that. I know what you mean, but people have to learn to respect the law, and this seems to be the only way people learn. At least Mitch doesn't have a family."

The marshal went in and sat down on the sofa. Barbara, knowing just how to please her husband, went into the other room, picked up Ellie, and took her out to John, making both father and daughter happy. After a nice dinner John and Barbara went in and sat on the sofa for a couple of hours and talked, before turning in.

The next morning, after Barbara changed his bandages and fixed breakfast for him, John went out to the barn, got his horse, and rode into town. He went into the office, relieved Carl, and went back to the cell-block to check on his prisoners. All three were sitting on the edge of their cots, waiting for the marshal to come in. He handcuffed them one at a time and, with Brett and Fred, led them down to the courthouse.

They turned over the jurisdiction to the federal marshals inside the courthouse. The three were taken down the hall where they would be cleaned up. Afterward deputies took them down to the courthouse and seated them in front of the judge's bench. The judge came in from a side door. After hearing the charges against the two men, the judge ordered their property be sold, and the proceeds given to the parents of the girl they had hurt. They were also sentenced to five years at Yuma Territorial Prison, with the possibility of three years being knocked off that sentence for good behavior.

The judge turned his attention to Mitch. After reading the notes, he noticed the marshal's recommendation. John wasn't sure which of the two men pulled the trigger. He pointed out that at twenty three, Mitch had a clean record.

The judge looked at Mitch. "Young man, you're charged with bank robbery resulting in the death of a peace officer. What's your plea?"

Mitch got to his feet. He kept his head down, and then looked up at the judge.

"I'm guilty Your Honor. Both my partner and I thought nobody would be around and we would be able to simply go into the bank and get the money. I'm sorry for what happened."

"Any time a peace officer is killed in the line of duty, everybody involved gets the death penalty. I may be making a mistake, but Marshal Green talked to me this morning in my chambers. You're sentenced to ten years hard labor at Yuma Territorial Prison. Don't make me regret this."

Mitch didn't know whether or not to be relieved. He looked at the judge and turned around and looked at John. Tears formed in his eyes as deputies led him away. The train going to Yuma would be coming in later that afternoon.

John, Brett, and Sam returned to the office. The three didn't say much of anything as they made their way back.

"Did you really ask for leniency for that bastard?" Brett said. "That doesn't sound like you."

John sat behind the desk. "I don't know why, but I don't think Mitch lied to me. I think he just got caught up in more than he could handle. Dan Dixon was a longtime friend of mine. At first I didn't think hanging would be good enough, but then I talked to Mitch a few times back there in the cell."

Brett nodded yes as he and Sam left the office. John sat back and thought about what had happened that morning. Minutes later the U.S. marshals brought the three prisoners back into the jail. John took them back, and locked them up. Mitch had an appreciative look in his eye as John walked out to get paperwork from the marshals. It would be several hours before the train arrived.

At noon, Barbara brought in lunch for the crew. She had left Ellie with friends. Sam, Brett, and Fred came into the office, and sat down to a fine lunch and coffee. During their lunch break, Loren came in with lunch for the three prisoners.

Loren stopped on his way out. "Word has it; the murderer isn't going to hang. Is that true?"

"You know Loren, if there were any proof which of those men pulled the trigger, I'd be first in line to pull the rope. I honestly feel his partner was the one that killed Danny. In most cases like these, it's true everybody involved would probably swing. I can't tell you why, but this case was different."

Loren shook his head from side to side and left the office. Barbara asked John about it, and quickly realized he didn't want talk about it. After lunch, and a little conversation, John went outside, helped his wife onto the buggy, and watched as she turned the buggy around and rode off down the street. The two deputies resumed their duties and the marshal went back into the office.

Later that afternoon, John went back to the cells to handcuff his prisoners and get them ready for transport. He then had Brett bring a buckboard around to the front of the office. Sam came over to help. The three prisoners were taken out of the office and tied to the buckboard. John followed the wagon on horseback.

They pulled into the train station, and the marshal went up to the Ticketmaster to arrange the transport to Yuma. The train had been due about a half hour before it finally arrived. John noticed the side of the mail-car had been blown off. He went over to the train's conductor.

"What happened, Corky?" John said. "Where's Joe?"

"Four men, with masks blocked the tracks just out of Taos, New Mexico," Corky said. "They blew the side of the mail car off with dynamite. Joe was inside. There's not much left of him. A couple of the passengers in one of the other cars got injured, but they'll survive."

John called over to Brett to go get the doctor and the undertaker. He and Sam then put the three outlaws on the train and handcuffed them to the seats. He walked up to the train's engineer.

"What can you tell me, Hank?"

"Not a hell of a lot," Hank said. "I noticed a tree had fallen across the tracks. When I stopped, Barney and I got out of the cab to go move it. As soon as we stepped down, two men with masks put their guns on us and ordered us to stay quiet. About a minute later I heard an explosion coming from the back of the train."

"How many were there?" John said. "Corky said there were four of them."

"I just saw the two of them marshal. I noticed one of the men was missing a finger, he had black hair. The other man looked kind of sandy-haired. I wish I could help you more."

"Are you both okay?"

"I'm a little shaken up. For what it's worth, they headed south toward the Mexican border."

The doctor and undertaker showed up together in the doctor's buckboard. Brett went over and helped the undertaker take the body out of the car and put it into the back of his wagon.

John went over to the pale and shaking conductor, who had pulled the records from the safe.

"Hello John, from what I can see here, there was over fifty thousand dollars' worth of gold in the strong boxes. I only saw four men, and they were all on horses. I suspect there was a fifth man somewhere there with a wagon, but I didn't see it."

John sent Brett on ahead to Yuma with the prisoners. Railroad officials disconnected the mail-car for closer inspection. Cases of mail were taken off and put in the baggage car before the train left. John climbed into the mail-car, and to the area where the strong boxes had been removed. Finding nothing, he returned to his office. Sam sat on the bench in front of the office when John got there. He knew there wasn't anything more he could do that night, so he left Sam in charge, and headed back to the farm.

Barbara came outside when she saw her husband walking back from the barn.

"Well, I take it you got your prisoners off okay. Your daughter's been a bit of an imp since I got her home."

"Oh, what's her problem? I thought girls didn't start acting that way until they got older."

"I think she just misses her daddy. Maybe you should go in and see what you can do with her while I get dinner on?"

John went over to the pump and cleaned up before going into the house. He heard Ellie, yelling in the back room. He went in, picked her up, and sat her on his lap.

"Well, young lady, what seems to be your problem?" He smiled at her.

She immediately laughed when her dad started stroking her tummy with her teddy bear. After a few minutes she calmed down, and John left the room. By that time Barbara had dinner on the table. The two of them sat down, said grace, and enjoyed a delicious dinner of fried rabbit. After dinner Barbara went back to the bedroom to nurse Ellie.

John sat on the sofa, thinking of the day's events. He'd already contacted the sheriffs in the border towns in case the bandits were dumb enough to cross there. He felt it more likely they would cross the river to get rid of any tracks they might leave. He decided to leave early in the morning, and take Al, an Apache and a deputy marshal with a gift for being able to track.

John went into the bedroom and lay down on the feather bed. About a half hour later, his wife came in and lay beside him.

"I'm probably going to get out of here before sunrise," John said. "I may be gone a couple of days. Carrying that much gold should slow them down quite a bit, especially going through that kind of country."

"Well, just be careful. Don't show up here with any more bullets in you."

The next morning, John got up, had a cup of coffee, saddled his horse and headed out. He had put on his warm coat due to the weather being cold. He met Al at the office. A few minutes later, Fred showed up as well. The three men headed out towards Mexico. John knew there were a limited number of places a wagon full of gold could cross the river as most of that area had trees and cactus but no usable trails.

"The most likely place they can cross will be between Nogales and Agua Prieta," John said. "We best split up. You two go to Agua Prieta, and ride toward Nogales. I'll go to Nogales and head towards you."

They got down within a few miles of the border and split up. John rode into Nogales and summoned the sheriff to get a posse together and head up on the Mexican side of the border. Being friends with the Marshal, the sheriff readily agreed. The marshal rode toward his meeting with the other deputies. A few miles up, he saw wagon tracks heading toward the river. Following them, he found the wagon stuck in the mud, and the outlaws desperately trying to move it. His other deputies hadn't shown up yet but not being in a hurry, he waited until they got there. They showed up a little later and followed John to the river.

The three lawmen came out from behind the trees with guns drawn and placed the outlaws under arrest. Seeing they outmanned the deputies, three of the outlaws drew their weapons. Their guns already out; the marshal and his deputies shot them dead. The other two put their hands over their heads and slowly walked to where the deputies stood.

The deputies hooked up their horses, along with those of the outlaws. They were able to pull the wagon out of the mud and to the top of the ravine. John handcuffed both his prisoners.

About that time, the deputies from Mexico came across the river. The marshal thanked them by giving them the outlaws' horses.

As the sun started to set, the deputies set up camp for the night. The weather began getting cold as darkness set in. The outlaws were fed hardtack and the deputies had bacon and eggs with coffee. They tied the outlaws around a tree, and pulled their bedrolls off the horses. Next morning, they again had a breakfast of bacon and eggs with coffee. This time they shared with the outlaws. Afterward, they allowed the men to go back into the trees and cactus to relieve themselves.

The handcuffed outlaws were unceremoniously thrown into the back of the wagon. The deputies headed back to Tucson following the wagon with Fred on the seat and his horse tied to the wagon. They arrived in Tucson, late that afternoon. Fred pulled up in front of the jail, unloaded the prisoners, and proceeded down to the train station with the gold.

John and Al took the prisoners inside and locked them up. They would be charged with armed robbery and murder. This time, John had no pity for either of them, as they both had long-time criminal records. John called on Deputy Carlos Rivera, who replaced Pete, the deputy sent to Tombstone, to stay at the jail for the night and relieve Sam. After doing the paperwork necessary for their trial, the marshal went back to the cells. Talking to them, he realized if given another chance, they would do exactly the same thing again. Neither showed remorse for the death of the agent in the mail car. John came back into the office.

"You know, Carlos, I don't understand men like that. I guess they think robbing and killing will make their life easier."

"Don't look at me marshal, I don't get it either. They would probably sell the gold in Mexico, and I doubt they could get much for it. It certainly wasn't worth risking their lives.—I'll watch them. Why don't you head home?"

"I think I'll do that, thank you," John said. "I'll see you in the morning."

John's horse, still saddled and hitched to the rail, looked tired. John stopped by the water trough, mounted him and headed for home. He rode to the barn, pulled off the saddle, and gave the horse an extra helping of oats. He pulled four apples off the tree outside, gave one to the other horse, and put three in the bucket with the oats.

Barbara waited for him on the front steps. She walked down and greeted her husband as he came from the barn. She gave him a loving kiss, and the two went into the house. After playing with his daughter, John went outside to the pump to get cleaned up and shaved. Barbara had fixed him a fine meal of fried chicken and biscuits. After dinner, John went in and lay on the bed, falling asleep almost immediately. Barbara went in and tended to Ellie. An hour later, she joined her husband on the bed.

The next morning, John slept in a little. Barbara got up, and nursed Ellie. She then fixed John a breakfast of ham and eggs, biscuits, and coffee. The smell of that breakfast cooking enticed John out of the bed and to the table. After breakfast, John went into the other room and put his daughter on his lap. She fell asleep shortly. John laid her down in her crib and came back out to the living room. He sat down for a half hour before going to the barn and saddling the other horse. He got back to the office a little later than usual. Fred had already taken over for Sam.

"Good morning, John," Fred said. "I didn't expect to see you here this early."

"I think I'd rather have stayed in bed today, but I'm getting to feel like that every day. Is everything going okay?"

"Yeah, I checked on the prisoners a while ago. Loren brought in breakfast for them. He just left before you got here."

Fred left the office, and John went to his desk. The circuit judge would be coming in that afternoon, and John had to finish the paperwork for the trial. He then went outside and sat on the bench with his feet up on the hitching-rail. The warm sun felt good.

Hearing a lot of noise, he walked over to the saloon down the street. He wanted to get there before it turned into a gunfight. He arrived just as one man by the batwing doors, pulled his gun on the other. Not risking a chance, John hit him on the head with the butt of his pistol and Jake came up from behind the bar.

"You sure timed that right," Jake said. "I'm sure he was about to shoot."

"What was that all about?" The marshal said. "It doesn't look like the other guy was even armed."

The man whose life John had just saved walked over to him. "I thank you, Marshal. I think he must've taken something I said wrong."

"Did anybody catch his name?"

"Ross was the only name I heard, Sheriff," a man at the bar said.

"By the way my name is Marshall John Green," he said to Jake. "Where's Zeke today?"

"I bought the place from him. I had a bar in Amarillo and moved here and went to work for him."

"I heard his wife was sick, maybe that's why I haven't seen him around for a while," the marshal said. "Well my office is just up the street. If you need anything or have any problems, just see me or one of my deputies. As you probably know, when cattle drives come through, it can get pretty rowdy in here."

"Oh don't I. Thank you Marshal."

John picked the man up off the floor, walked him to the jail and put him in a cell. A few minutes later, Loren came in with lunch a little early, as John had told him to do. He had also asked Barbara to bring their lunches in after the trial.

"I see you have another prisoner in here, Marshal. I have to run over and get another lunch. I'll be back in a few minutes."

John gave the three men their lunches and told them to eat fast. He went out to his desk, gathered the paperwork he'd prepared, and went outside to sit in the cool air. Loren came over with the other lunch, took it into the jail and came back out minutes later.

A half hour later, Fred came over to help John with the prisoners, and Carlos showed up to watch the jail. The marshal went back to the cellblock. The two deputies followed him.

"Okay, men, I want each of you, one at a time, to come up to the cell door."

After handcuffing the three, John and Fred took them out and loaded them onto a buckboard from the livery stable. Carlos stayed to watch the office. Getting to the courthouse, John turned the prisoners over to the deputy marshals in the hallway. The three were taken down the hall to be cleaned up and brought back to the courtroom. Fred went back to his duties, and John sat down at the prosecution table. The three men were brought in before the judge walked in.

"I've looked over the affidavits from the gold robbery on the train. I have little doubt the death of the man guarding the mail-car and conductors were totally premeditated. Do you have anything to say before I pronounce sentence?" The judge said.

"We didn't mean to hurt anybody judge, we just wanted the gold."

The judge sentenced both to hang, adding "May God have mercy on your souls."

The prisoners were taken back down the hall and from there, John and the deputies took the two back to the jail.

The next day, a preacher and witnesses stood near the gallows behind the building. About 30 spectators stood in front of the structure. Some had brought their families and a lunch basket. The two men were taken up the thirteen steps of the gallows, where the minister said a few words before covers were placed over their heads. The two started yelling and were in tears as the hangman pulled the lever. Their feet shortly went still. John bowed his head for a few seconds, and then motioned for the undertaker to come over and pick up the dead bodies.

John returned to his office. Executions like this gave John no pleasure; however he realized the necessity for it. He went inside and put up his guns. His deputies and wife were there having lunch. John wasn't hungry after the morning's proceedings, so he held his daughter while the other three finished their meal.

The circuit judge stayed in Tucson that night to pass sentence on the man in the gunfight at the saloon that morning. After Barbara and Ellie left for home, John finished his paperwork on that case. When his deputy relieved him that afternoon, John walked over to the saloon, sat at the bar and ordered a beer.

"Zeke, do you remember anything more about that fight this morning?"

"There wasn't much to tell. According to the guy he was going to shoot, it was unprovoked. Truthfully, when I turned around, that's when you walked in. I'm pretty sure we would've had a dead man in here if you hadn't."

"Was he liquored up?"

"Like I said this morning, I was about ready to ask him to leave. I was busy, so I let it go."

"The judge is staying at his ranch overnight for a trial in the morning. I can let him know what you said, so I don't think he'll need you."

"I appreciate that, Marshal. I get nervous when I talk to those guys. Oh, I almost forgot your beer."

The marshal had one beer before heading for home. Afterward, he got his horse from the stable. The animal had been groomed, fed, and watered. The stable-man saddled the horse when he saw John coming. John thanked him and headed back to the farm. He took the horse into the barn, and walked into the house expecting to see his wife and daughter, but they weren't there. He walked out to the barn, and saw no sign of the buggy, or any evidence that it had been there.

Thinking his wife had probably made a trip to the general store, and got talking to somebody, he didn't worry. He went over to the pump, got cleaned up, and went into the house. After a couple of hours, John realized something must have happened to his family. He saddled his horse and headed back to Town. He and three deputies checked all of the stores in and out of town. John had apparently been the last one to see his wife and child.

John got hold of Al, an ex-Indian tracker and deputy marshal. John felt if anybody could find his family, it would be Al. Getting dark, John realized tracking that buggy would not be easy. Luckily, Al had been known for being able to track at night. The marshal and his deputy met in the office at dusk.

"This is the last place I saw them, Al," John said. "It was about 3 o'clock this afternoon."

Chapter 3

"The buggy track is pretty clear here. As long as it stays on dirt trails, we should be able to at least get an idea of the direction it headed."

"Barbara never would have done something like this without checking with me first," John said. "I'm sure whoever did this isn't going to make it easy to find them."

About that time, Carlos came out of the office and over to John.

"John, I found this note inside one of the cells when I went in to clean it."

"Marshal, *if you want to see your wife and daughter alive again, you'll let Ross out.*"

John went into the cell that held his prisoner. "Ross, if anything happens to my wife and daughter, I'm going to hold you personally responsible."

"Look, Marshal, I don't have any idea what you're talking about."

The marshal figured the man probably knew more than he would be willing to say, but he didn't have time to question him any further. He went out, and with Al, started following the tracks. Carlos had other ideas. He handcuffed the prisoner and pulled him back behind the jail. He aimed his gun at the man's foot.

"Okay, where are they? Don't pretend you don't know what I'm talking about."

"You're a lawman, you know you can't use that thing on me," Ross said, with a grin.

Carlos pulled the trigger and moved the gun up a foot. Ross started screaming in agony.

Ross yelled, "I'll have your badge for that."

"I asked you a question. Where are they?"

Again, Ross refused to answer and Carlos pulled the trigger. Ross screamed as pain shot up his leg.

"I'm going to go right up your leg, shoot your pleasure tool, and then go down the other one," Carlos said. "I have smelling salts for when you pass out."

About a second later, Ross yelled out, "Carl Bailey—he's got them out on his ranch," Ross said. "Please help me, get me a doctor."

"Let me assure you, Ross, if you're not telling the truth, I'll come back and finish the job."

Carlos took the prisoner in, handcuffed him inside the cell next to the cot and tied a bandanna around his leg. The deputy went for the doctor, and gave him a key to the cell. Carlos went outside, mounted up and raced to catch up with John and Al.

"John," Carlos said, "Barbara and Ellie are out at Bailey's ranch. I think they're okay, but you better get out there fast."

The marshal left Al to continue tracking, just in case it turned out to be a false lead. John ran his horse at full gallop to the ranch, and made his way up to the bunkhouse with his gun drawn. He didn't see his wife or daughter, but saw the buggy behind the main house. He made his way to a back window of the ranch house and, to his great relief, saw Ellie playing on the bed. The marshal slowly made his way around to the front door.

One of the ranch hands thought he saw something, and came out of the bunkhouse to investigate. John saw him first. He aimed his gun at the man, ordered him to come over, and slowly walk in the front door of the house.

Bailey sat at the table with his wife. "What's up, Juan?" The man turned white when he saw the marshal come in behind his employee. Barbara looked at her husband from her chair against the wall, in disbelief. Keeping his gun aimed at the table, John pulled out his knife and cut his wife's bonds. She got up and ran to the back room to get their daughter, while John handcuffed Bailey. Bailey's wife kept still.

"Juan, get your boss a horse. Tell the men in the bunkhouse to stay there, if they don't want to go to jail."

John put Bailey on the horse, handcuffing him to the saddle horn. The two men followed the buggy back to town. John could see Al coming down the trail.

"Thanks, Al, you can come back with us," John said. "The girls are fine."

Later when the six got back to Tucson, Barbara and Ellie took the buggy back to the farm. John and Al brought the prisoner to the jail and saw the doctor leaving as they rode up.

"What's going on, Doc?" John said. "Is something wrong in there?"

"It's just an accidental shooting, nothing to worry about."

John walked back to the cell and saw his prisoner bandaged up. He walked to a back cell where he saw Carlos sitting," The marshal asked, "Did you do that?"

"I'm not in here for nothing you know. Ross isn't a very nice guy."

John summoned Carlos off the cot, and out to the office where both men sat down.

"You know we can get in a lot of trouble for what you did. I'll talk to the judge in the morning. Knowing him, I have a feeling he may think it was justified."

"I went back there to talk to Ross," the deputy said. "The more I talked and listened to his smart Alec answers, the more fed up I got with him. I don't know where the idea of doing that to him came from, but truthfully, I'm not sorry I did it."

"I can imagine. Thank you," John said, shaking his hand. "Do you want me to get somebody else to fill in for you tonight?"

"No, I'm pretty well wired. I can handle it. You go on home. You've had a rough day."

John thanked Carlos, went out, mounted up, and headed back to the farm. When he got there Barbara had already put Ellie to bed, and although late, she'd fixed a nice meal for herself and John. Afterward they cleaned up and went to bed.

The next morning John got up to the smell of bacon and eggs. After breakfast and coffee, John kissed his wife and went out to the barn and saddled a horse.

John relieved Carlos the next morning when he got to the office, and got the paperwork ready for court that morning. Loren brought in an early breakfast of oatmeal, toast and coffee for the two prisoners, as John had to have time to get them ready for court.

Brett arrived a little later when the train came into the station. His horse had been saddled and brought up from the stable earlier that morning. He rode the horse to the office, tied it to the hitching-rail, and went inside.

"Good morning Boss," Brett said. "Is there anything going on?"

"Hi, Brett, just get in?" John said. "We have a couple of prisoners to take into court this morning," Brett poured himself a cup of coffee and relaxed.

"I guess there's no hurry."

About an hour later, John and Brett went back to the cells. John ordered the two men over to the bars, to be handcuffed. He and Brett took them out to a waiting buckboard and down to the courthouse. After releasing the men into the custody of the deputies there, John and Brett went in and took a chair in front of the bench. The two prisoners were brought in, and sat at a table next to the lawmen. A couple of minutes later the judge came in.

He called Ross to the table, where a deputy swore him in. "Mr. Ross, you're charged with the robbery of a train's mail-car and, with the murder of the guard in charge of the gold the train carried. What's your plea?"

"There were five of us. I didn't kill anyone. I just got caught."

"Do you realize, if you are caught in the commission of a robbery, resulting in anybody's death, you are guilty of murder? Do you have anything to say before sentencing?"

"No, Your Honor, I don't. I didn't mean to shoot the guy."

Ross caught himself as soon as he said that. He turned red in the face as he looked at the judge.

"I sentence you to be taken from the courthouse, to the jail and tomorrow morning, hanged by the neck until you are dead."

A deputy removed Ross from the courtroom. The judge said, "Next case". Bailey took the seat Ross had just vacated.

"Mr. Bailey, you're charged with the kidnapping of Marshal Green's wife and daughter, and threatening the life of both of them. I read the note that was left in the jail cell. How do you plea?"

"I never would've hurt the marshal's family. I was just trying to help my friend. Neither his wife or daughter were hurt."

"I understand you had his wife tied up, and the baby in a separate room. I wish I had the authority to send you to the gallows for that, but I sentence you to five years of hard labor at the Yuma territorial prison."

Deputies took Bailey out of the courtroom. John felt his sentence to be a little harsh, and told the judge so. The judge agreed that he could be let out for good behavior, but would still serve a minimum of three years. John and Brett picked up Ross from the courtroom and transported him and Bailey back to the jail. Sam came out of the jail, and took Ross and Bailey back to one of the cells.

The next morning John and Brett took Ross to the gallows behind the jail. The marshal took Ross up the thirteen steps, and placed a noose around his neck. The preacher gave him last rites, and the hangman placed the hood over Ross's head. The spectators watched as the hangman pulled the lever, snapping the outlaw's neck. A couple of men took the body down to the undertaker's buckboard, and he took it to his office.

John went into the office shortly before his wife showed up with lunch for him and his two deputies. She walked back to the cell that held Bailey. He looked at her, and turned his head. Barbara didn't say anything; she just turned around and walked into the office, where she opened the lunch basket. She handed each of the men a roast beef sandwich, and potato salad.

"It never fails to amaze me how these sandwiches keep improving," Sam said. "The same goes for the tater salad."

"Well, I'm glad you enjoy it," Barbara said. "Has Loren come in yet?"

"Not yet," John said. "We were sure we would only need one, but there was always the possibility the judge would give him a stay. Loren was at the hanging, so I imagine he'll be here pretty quick. Where's that daughter of mine?"

"I left Ellie down the street with a couple of the ladies. I didn't think listening to you guys talk about the hanging would be the best thing for her."

About that time Loren came in with lunch for Bailey. Barbara offered to take the lunch back to Bailey. She had a few things to say to him, and took it back and shoved it under the bars. He looked at her.

"I just want to say, I know you were just trying to help your friend," Barbara said. "I appreciate you not hurting me or my daughter. I really like to think the threatening letter, was just that!"

Bailey apologized to her. She walked out of the cell and into John's office. The men continued discussing the morning's events. Cleaning up after lunch, Barbara left. John walked her out, kissed her, and helped her onto the buggy. He watched in pride as she turned the buggy around and rode off down the dusty street.

A couple of fights in the saloon a couple miles away, kept Al and Brett busy that afternoon. While down there, the deputies checked in on the assay office, and three banks. As none of them had any trouble over the last few months, everything seemed quiet. The general store and a few other places were checked as well. They got back to the office in the late afternoon.

Carlos showed up to relieve John, who waited for Al and Brett to return to the office. Both men wrote reports on the saloon fights.

"Damages to the saloon were minor. Both men paid the barkeep," Brett said. "The other fight involved one of the ladies of the night. She was pretty badly beaten by one of her customers. He's back in a cell. His name is Jarvis. We didn't lay a hand on him, but I sure felt like it."

John walked down to the stable where his horse had been fed, watered, and saddled. The music from Jake's place had lightened his mood. He rode to his farm, put the horse in the barn and went to the house, stopping by the pump on his way. Barbara had dinner ready for him when he came in. She threw her arms around him and gave him a loving kiss. She suggested he may want to go back and see his daughter before dinner.

She played with her toy bear when he opened her bedroom door, and got excited when she saw him come in.

"Well how's my girl today?" John said, picking up Ellie out of the playpen he had made for her. She started giggling as he rubbed her tummy. He then put her down, went out, and sat down to join his wife for dinner.

"The girls seemed to enjoy their time with Ellie this afternoon, and she's been in a good mood."

"I'm still a little shaky over the two of you being kidnapped. I now realize, Carl had no intention of hurting either of you, but I didn't know it at the time. It made me realize how much you two mean to me."

After a meal of baked squab, with all the trimmings, Barbara went into Ellie's bedroom and nursed her, and put her down for the night. She returned to the living room and sat down on the couch. John had put a couple of logs in the fireplace and got a fire going. She moved over and joined him on the couch and leaned over putting her head down on his lap. A little foreplay on the sofa escalated into a lovemaking session on the feather bed. The two fell asleep in each other's arms.

The next morning John went to the office where he would need to fill out the paperwork for Jarvis's trial. Getting there, he relieved Carlos. Brett and Sam came in a few minutes later.

"I'm afraid Jarvis is going to have to stay in jail," Brett said. "I guess until the judge sobers up a bit."

"Do you have any idea how long that's going to take?" John said.

"I can't say, John, he's over at Jake's place practically passed out."

"That doesn't sound like Bart," John said. "He must be having trouble with his wife again. I thought they'd straightened that out."

"I told Loren to figure on bringing breakfast, lunch, and probably dinner for Jarvis today."

The marshal left the office and walked over to Jake's saloon to try to send the judge home for the day. John went in and saw Bart sitting at a rear table, facing the door. He called Zeke over.

"How long has this been going on," John said. "I need him for a trial this morning."

"I'm afraid that's not going to happen, John," Zeke said. "He's been here since early this morning. That's his second pint."

John walked over to the judge's table. He sat down across from the judge, and took the bottle away from him. The judge barely reacted.

"Bart, you know I needed you in that courtroom this morning. It's too late to get a circuit judge in here now, so I guess we'll have to put off the trial until tomorrow morning. I think I better take you home so you can clean up"

"Come on, John, you know I'm not drunk," Bart said, slurring his words repeatedly.

He could barely walk, as John and a couple of his deputies escorted the judge out to his carriage. After tying his horse to the carriage, Brett got up on the seat with the judge. John and Sam went back to the office. Sam left to patrol the area, and John went back to see Billy Jarvis.

"Well Billy, looks like you're going to have to enjoy our hospitality in here for another day. The judge is indisposed this morning, and probably won't be able to get back to the courtroom until tomorrow."

Jarvis looked at him as if he could care less, then turned around, and lay back on the bunk. The marshal walked to his desk, finished filling out the report on his prisoner, and went outside. The weather had cooled down a bit over the last couple of days. A sandstorm made a mess of the sidewalks.

John sat on the seat, putting his feet up on the rail. About that time, he saw the stage coming in at full gallop from Amarillo. When the stage stopped at the livery, John realized something had happened. Then Sam came running up from the doctor's office.

"John, the stage coach was robbed about thirty miles back. Bubba tried to stop the robbery; they shot him while he sat on the seat, and made off with the strongbox. Two of the passengers in the coach were shot and killed as well. For some reason, they didn't kill the driver, but they did shoot him. I guess they didn't check to be sure they had killed him."

"That was pretty stupid of them. They had to realize he could identify them."

"They were wearing masks," Sam said. "Steve, the driver thinks he may know one of them, but he's in and out of consciousness right now."

John went over to the doc's office, hoping Steve would be able to give him a little information on exactly where the outlaws went. The marshal figured it would have to be fairly close to where they stopped the stage. He went into the doc's office and saw the man lying unconscious.

"Doc, I need to ask Steve a few questions."

"I gave him a sedative, but I have smelling salts here. I can bring him back for a while, but he'll be in a lot of pain."

"I need to find the location," John said. "It was stopped about fifty miles from here."

The doc pulled a bottle off a nearby shelf. He took off the cap and put the bottle under Steve's nose. He started to flinch and cough before coming to. John realized this would be painful for him.

"Steve, I realize this happened about fifty miles east of town. Do you remember any landmarks or nearby trails, especially heading toward Mexico?"

Steve mumbled, "Looked like they might be heading toward Tombstone, that's about all I can tell you." Steve again fell into unconsciousness.

John went back to the office, telling Sam to find Al and meet him at the stable. A few minutes later, the three left for Tombstone. They rode about fifty miles east before turning south up the mountain for another twenty miles. The outlaws had left deep tracks from carrying the strongbox full of gold. Their tracks stopped at the Birdcage Inn. The marshal had Sam and Al go inside the saloon and wait for him. He then went to the Sheriff's office to see Pete, and let him know what they were doing. Pete put on his gun belt and walked down to the saloon with John. Sam and Al had gone to the bartender, and found their quarry at a back table, gambling. They made their way past the mirrored bar and came to that table.

Thinking they'd killed everybody and made a clean getaway, neither man worried about the Marshal coming in. That soon changed when they found four guns aimed at them. The others were told to leave the gambling table, leaving the stakes on the table. John put the two scruffy men in cuffs and took them over to the jail. The circuit judge would be coming in the next morning. John and Pete joined Al and Sam at the inn for a beer and a sandwich before the three lawmen from Tucson headed for home.

Early that evening the three arrived back into town from Tombstone. The weather turned cold as John rode east, heading to his farm. He told the deputies he would handle the paperwork in the morning.

When Barbara saw a cloud of dust and heard the horse coming, she started dinner. John put the horse up for the night, giving him water, oats and a couple of apples. He went to the pump and cleaned up before going in the house. Barbara came over and gave him a longing kiss. He went to the back room to see Ellie. She beamed as he walked through the door of her bedroom. John picked her up.

"How's my little girl doing? " John said, picking her up. "Have you been behaving yourself today?" He put her down in her crib.

She looked up at her dad, and then showed him her toy bear. John bent over and patted her on the forehead, rubbed her tummy a little, and left the room.

"I just can't get enough of that daughter of ours," John said, pulling Barbara to him. "Or you either, for that matter."

The two embraced in a warm kiss and hug before sitting down for dinner. Knowing he would be tired after the long ride, Barbara had fixed her husband fried chicken and biscuits. After dinner John went into the living room while Barbara cleaned up. Later she brought in a bottle of wine, and the two enjoyed each other's company for the rest of the evening.

The next morning John left early for the cold dusty ride into town, he had worn a warm overcoat. The marshal had paperwork from the day before and an appointment with the judge, providing Bart had taken his advice and sobered up. The marshal took his horse into the stable, told Cecil he would need the buckboard a little later, and then walked down to the office.

Brett and Loren came up from the cellblock. Jarvis had been fed, and made ready for transport. After filling out the paperwork from the day before, he asked Brett to handcuff Jarvis before leaving for home. Al and Sam came into the office shortly afterward. Sam went to the cellblock, and brought Jarvis out to the waiting buckboard in front of the jail. John came out and put Al in charge of the jail. The marshal and his deputy left for the county courthouse.

A dust storm came up earlier and the weather began to warm up. They took their prisoner in, and two marshals took him down the hall to get cleaned up and ready for court. Sam went back and sat in the audience, while John took a seat at the table in front of the judge. Bart came in, stone sober.

After reading John's affidavit, the judge looked at Jarvis and asked him if he had anything to say.

"The whore had it coming. She tried to steal money from my wallet, and I caught her. It made me mad."

"Well Mr. Jarvis, I happen to know Wanda-sue very well," The judge said without thinking, which got a few chuckles from the audience. "She is definitely not a thief."

Billy looked down. He knew he lied, so did the judge. "I'm sorry, Your Honor, it won't happen again."

Bart looked at him. "Not at least for the next couple of years. A despicable act like that is one thing, but lying to me under oath is another. I sentence you to two years hard labor at the Arizona State prison."

John got up. He and Sam took Jarvis out to the buckboard. They returned it to the stable after turning their prisoner over to Al. They walked to the restaurant across the street from the jail.

"Well, Loren, it doesn't look like we have much business for you today. I guess the least I can do is get coffee for me and Sam. I'll need lunch for Jarvis at noon, but that's about it. The stage is due in at one o'clock."

"I'll make it a little early today," Loren said.

At about noon, Barbara showed up with sandwiches for the lawmen. John held Ellie on his lap while they had lunch. She always enjoyed being bounced on her father's knee. She kept trying to make a grab for his sandwich, which delighted him. Once in a while he gave her a little bite of bread when his wife wasn't looking. Loren came in with lunch for Billy Jarvis, and took it back to his cell. He came back a couple of minutes later.

"Well, John, I guess I may or may not see you tomorrow."

"Thanks, Loren, we'll let you know."

John helped his wife and daughter out to the buggy, and watched as it turned around and rolled down the street toward the farm. He still remembered the week before, when it would be the last he saw of them for a couple of days. He walked back into the office. Al and Sam returned to their duties outside, and John went in to see his prisoner.

"You know, Billy, the judge would have gone a lot easier on you if you'd just told the truth in the first place. Why did you beat up on Wanda Sue?"

"I don't know. I just enjoy that sort of thing. It just went a little too far this time, I guess."

John handcuffed his prisoner and took him out to the bench in front of the jail.

A short time later the stagecoach showed up and John put his prisoner inside and handcuffed him to the ring, put there for that purpose.

"How's Steve getting along?" the driver asked. "I understand he got held up near the road to Tombstone. I pay special attention to that area when I go through there."

"Steve's doing okay. Both of those guys were hanged this morning up in Tombstone. At least you won't have to worry about them, and it may make others think twice before trying it."

The driver pulled the reins. "I doubt it, but let's hope so. See you later, John." The marshal watched as the stagecoach headed to the train station, to drop off passengers and mail before the long dusty trip to Phoenix.

The marshal returned to the office. Being a slow afternoon, he went outside to the bench in front of the jail to enjoy the warmth of the sun. Soon Carlos showed up at the office, and relieved him. Sam and Al soon returned to the office as well. Brett came in for the night shift, and the other four deputies left for home.

The marshal felt tired when he got home that night. After taking care of the horse, he stopped at the pump, and saw Barbara on the porch, with Ellie in her arms. He went to the pump, got cleaned up, then walked up, kissed his wife and daughter. He took Ellie, and went in the open door to his daughter's bedroom.

After playing with her for a few minutes, John came out to a delightful dinner of chicken and dumplings. Fresh peach pie and coffee rounded out the meal nicely. After cleaning up, the two went into the living room and to the sofa. Ellie began to cry in the back room. Barbara went in to nurse their daughter. In the meantime, John got the fire going in the fireplace, then went back to the sofa, and waited for his wife to return.

Shortly, Barbara returned to her husband on the sofa. They cuddled and enjoyed the warmth of the fire. Some of their discussions centered on the case of the beating of Wanda sue.

Barbara looked up at her husband. "I can't understand what causes men like that to want to hurt women."

"It's hard to say. I sure see enough of it."

John told his wife of Bart's faux-pas in court. She got a laugh out of that. The rest of the evening they just continued to cuddle.

The next morning, being Sunday, they dressed Ellie, and took the buggy to the church in town. The weather turned nice with a light wind blowing. Barbara had packed a few things for lunch down by Lake Tanganyika. After the service, all the women insisted on holding Ellie. The minister and several other men came over to see the marshal.

They always enjoyed swapping tales, mostly about their wives or the weather. John and his family got onto the buggy and went to their favorite picnic spot near the lake. After lying on the blanket and nursing their daughter, Barbara put out a fine spread for them. The marshal and his wife enjoyed a nice meal after getting coffee from the small campfire, and feeding and watering the horse. These Sunday afternoon outings were always special to them. They gave John a much needed rest and Barbara enjoyed talking to her husband in the tranquility of the surrounding area.

Early that evening, John packed up the buggy, and the three returned to their farm. He lifted his wife and daughter down from the buggy and onto the porch. He took the buggy to the stable, put it away, and gave the horse a couple of apples. He also gave an apple to their other horse.

He came into the house, put his hat up, and went in to change clothes. He could hear Ellie laughing with her mother in the other room. He lay down on the bed, and waited for his wife to come in. A few minutes later he fell into a light sleep. Barbara came in and, not wanting to disturb him, went out to the living room. She threw a couple of logs into the fireplace and started a fire. She then lay back on the couch and fell asleep.

John woke up when he heard his daughter getting restless in the other room. He went in to see her and gave her the stuffed animal she had dropped on the floor. He went to the living room to find his wife asleep on the couch. She soon awoke. Having had the heavy lunch that day, John didn't feel hungry, and after Barbara had a sandwich, the two went to bed.

The next morning, after breakfast, John went out to the barn, saddled his horse, and headed to town. There, he stabled the horse and walked down to his office. Carlos slept on John's chair, and awoke when the marshal came in.

"Everything okay this morning, Carlos?"

"We have a few customers in the cells. We had a murder yesterday morning over in front of Jake's. Both men had been drinking, and I guess they made a bet on who was the fastest draw. The winner is back in one of the cells. The other two got drunk and started a fight in the saloon down the street. They're just sleeping it off."

"It sounds like you had a busy Sunday," John said. "Go on home, and get some sleep. I'll see you later."

Soon after Carlos left, Brett and Al came into the office. Sam and a couple of the other deputies were out on their rounds. Al went back to check on the prisoners, returned, and poured him and the marshal a cup of coffee.

"The two guys that started the fight in the saloon the other night are still in there snoring. The other man is sitting on his bunk crying like a baby. I guess him and the man he shot and killed in the saloon last night were best of friends."

"Under those circumstances, and the fact that both men were drunk and agreed to the dual, the judge will probably go a little easy on him. Being friends, it sounds like something he's going to have to live with for the rest of his life."

"The schoolmarm was in here yesterday afternoon after church," Brett said. "I guess somebody's been breaking in the schoolhouse and stealing things. The town sheriff didn't want anything to do with it. She just wants you to talk to him."

"Did she say what kind of things?"

"No, but I guess it was just school supplies and stuff like that."

"I'll stop down there a little later on today," John said. "I may need her help with Ellie in a few years."

The men sat and discussed some of the serious problems that had occurred over the last several months at Jake's. Most of these involved the cattlemen that came through resulting in drunken fights. The other bars didn't seem to be having that many problems. John thought it probably had something to do with Jake being closer to the stage line and the railroad. He decided to have a talk with Jake about it, and see if they couldn't come to an agreement. Perhaps a deputy could be stationed there when it got busy.

About that time, the stage from Phoenix showed up at the stables. The driver was seriously wounded and three men inside the coach had been killed. Cecil called Al from up the street over to the stables. He sent a young man up to the jail to let John know what happened. John strapped on his gun and holster, and went to the stable. Doc pronounced the four men dead, and the undertaker loaded them onto his wagon as John and Brett arrived.

"They were all killed with Chippewa Indian arrows," Al said. "The driver scratched the word "Indians" on the seat, before he passed out."

"That makes no sense. Those people are peaceful," John said. "We've never had trouble with them. Besides they're mostly up north."

The stable hand jumped up on the coach and rolled it inside.

He told the marshal, "I think I better hold off on changing the horses until I hear from Don at the stagecoach company."

Brett rode down to the company's office and went inside.

"Don, I'm afraid I have bad news. The stage just showed up at the stable. Terry is in and out of consciousness and the passengers were killed. Terry scratched the word, "Indians" into the seat before he passed out. The strongbox was emptied. Chippewa arrows were used to kill the passengers and wound the driver."

"That doesn't make any sense, Brett," Don said. "We've always had a good relationship with the Indians. Besides that, the Chippewa tribes are mostly up in the Northwest and into Canada, but we do see a few here. We do most of their shipping of wares they make by coach, and rail especially, coming into the train station."

"I think John's aware of that, but I'll let him know anyway." Brett said, leaving the office.

Brett met John in his office a little later. John told Al to watch the office and call Carlos in case they didn't get back by nightfall and to let Barbara know , when she brought in the lunches, that he might not be back that evening.

The two men rode the dusty trail to the Pima reservation and had a talk with the Indian chief there. As John suspected, none of his people would have had anything to do with robbery and murder. He could not explain why the word "Indians" had been inscribed on the seat. The women of the tribe put up a good meal for John and Brett before they left the reservation.

The two men rode out to the Yaqui Indian reservation. They were basically told the same thing. Tribal elders were not aware of anyone in the tribe wishing to do the white man any harm. John and Brett were told the same by the elders at the Chippewa and Apache reservation where the two were asked to stay for dinner and given a tent for the night, as it began to get cold and dark.

The next morning, John and Brett got an early start after hot coffee and hardtack. It became obvious to both John and

Brett that somebody had dressed up in Indian garb and held up the stage with bows and arrows, hoping Indians would be blamed.

The marshal had an idea. He and Brett turned off to the south and headed up the hill to Tombstone. They went into the marshal's office and saw Pete.

"We had another stagecoach robbery down below the mountain," John said. "We believe the men may have come up here. They were carrying the strongbox, and we noticed deep horse tracks on our way up."

"I'll check with a couple of the deputies," Pete said. "Maybe they know something. Do you think our guys may have gone to the Birdcage Inn?"

"It's possible Brett. Why don't you go nose around up there and see what you can find out. See if anybody has been spending or losing a lot of money."

Chapter 4

John and Pete walked up the street to talk to the town's deputies. They found Bob at the courthouse, and Frankie at the "OK Corral". Both men would be ready if they were needed. John and Pete went to all the saloons in town but, talking to the bartenders found nobody spending a lot of money. The horse tracks led to the livery stable at the OK corral. The blacksmith said cowboys on horseback brought him a load of horseshoes. This explained the extra weight. John and Brett returned to Tucson.

After reaching town, John sent deputies to the M&M, Divinity, Congress Hall, and Brown's saloons. They were looking for anybody gambling and spending a large amount of money or gold. In the meantime John went to see the doctor about the type of arrows.

"Doc, what can you tell me about those arrows? I checked with the various Indian tribes around here. Brett picked up one of each while we went to the reservations, hoping maybe one of them might match."

"They're definitely Chippewa, but that makes no difference. I found lead under the arrows. The men were shot with forty-five slugs first, and the arrows put in the bullet-holes afterward. Somebody wants you to blame the Indians for this."

This put a whole new light on the case. John got back to his office where Sam waited for him.

"We checked the other saloons in town. I think our guys are at the Divinity. There are a couple of guys in there that got drunk and started mouthing off about pulling the wool over the eyes of the law. I asked the barkeep, and he told me they would be heading out of town this morning."

"Brett, I think we better go to the train station with Sam and check it out," John said. "Sam, did the barkeep say anything else about the guys?"

"Only laughing and bragging about getting out of town, and heading to California."

"I doubt they'd take the stage. If they have the money, they'll probably go by train. Did you get any kind of a description on these guys, Sam?"

"The barkeep did say something about a scar on the jaw of one of the two men."

"Let's go," John said. "There shouldn't be too many men with that type of scar."

The lawmen rode to the train station as the train began to leave, going north-west. John and the deputies jumped on the back, nearly being blown off by a sandstorm as the train pulled out. Not wanting to give away what they knew, Brett went into one of the passenger cars, walking forward and then back in order to see the faces of the passengers. He pulled his gun out before either of the men had a chance to react.

Sam went to the coal-car, jumped on it and told the engineer to stop the train. He explained the reason, and the engineer backed up to the station. By that time John and Brett had the two handcuffed. They took the men and their luggage off the train. Searching it, they found gold coin and cash with consecutive serial numbers matching those stolen.

"What are you doing, Marshal?" one of the men said. "We made that money fair and square. How do you know it was the money stolen from the stage?"

"Who said anything about the stage?" Brett said. "Did you say anything John?"

"Not that I recall. Come on, you two, you're going to have a nice comfortable cell tonight, which will be a lot nicer than what we've had to sleep on the last couple of nights because of you."

As the wind continued to blow, Sam showed up with a buckboard. The deputies put their two prisoners on it for transport back to the jail. They took the two outlaws in and put them behind bars, while Sam returned the buckboard to the stable. Barbara had just gotten to the office when John came in.

She laid Ellie on his desk. Brett walked across the street to let Loren know they would need a couple more lunches that day.

John picked up his daughter while Barbara put the lunches out for him and the deputies. Loren came in shortly with lunches for the prisoners. He later came out to the office, a little shaken.

"John, that prisoner, without the scar you've got in the cell, is my older brother, Frank. I can't believe he had anything to do with this."

"I'm sorry, Loren, but I'm afraid he has. The money stolen was found in the suitcases of both him and his partner."

Loren walked out of the jail in disbelief. John looked at the others in the office, including his wife, and shook his head. He would like to believe Loren's brother had nothing to do with this, but he knew the guy did. The judge would be holding trial the next morning, and after Barbara left, John spent the afternoon getting the necessary paperwork ready for their trial. Loren wanted to come over for a visit and John saw no reason not to let him.

Sam came in a little later to relieve John. By that time Loren had already left. The marshal told Sam about the prisoners, and left the office to get his horse. The animal had been saddled and ready to go when John got there. Getting to the farm, John put the animal in his stall, and picked a few apples for him, and the other horse. He went to the pump to get cleaned up and shaved before going in the house. The weather had turned cold and windy, picking up dust.

Barbara had just put Ellie down in the back room, and worked in the kitchen getting dinner ready. John came in, patted her on the rump, and went back to see his daughter before she went to sleep. Ellie looked up at her dad when he walked into the bedroom, put her arms and legs up and started squealing. John went over and pushed down on her stomach. She always seemed to enjoy that. After a few minutes he tucked her toy bear under her, and pulled the blanket up. He then went out to the dining room and had dinner. Afterward they went into the other room, where Barbara had a fire going. The two cuddled up before going to bed.

The next morning John got up a little early in order to get the three prisoners down to the courthouse. He rode into town, tipping his hat to some of the ladies on the sidewalk. He walked in the office, and saw Sam in his chair.

"Would you like a cup of coffee Sam?" John said. "It looks like we'll have a busy morning."

Sam didn't respond. John walked over and set the coffee on the desk. He went around the desk to shake his deputy, and got no response. He noticed a bad bruise on the back of Sam's head, and immediately went down and got the doctor.

"Something hit him," Doc said." He's dead."

John immediately went back to the cells, noticing the doors were open. One of the men lay dead on his cot. The two men holding up the stage were gone. John went out to the office, where the doctor summed a couple men to move Sam to the undertaker. Brett came in shortly after. John left him in charge of the office, and called Al in. The marshal's saw horse tracks going northeast.

"John, the man in the other cell was shot dead, where did they get the gun?" AL said. "And why would they shoot Josh, there's no way he could've gotten to them being locked in that cell."

"They probably didn't want a witness," The Marshal said. "I hate to say this, but our most likely suspect is Loren. One of the men is his brother."

With Al being an expert tracker, they were soon on the trail of the two men. Once the two men got past any likely path off the road, they surmised that the outlaws would try to hide out either in New Mexico, or Mexico. They figured they'd see tracks when they got there. They met up with the Overland stage about thirty miles out of town. The driver told John that he saw three men, in full gallop, some twenty miles back.

The marshals continued on a few miles, John saw a man lying at the side of the road. They stopped to investigate. Loren lay there with an obvious rattlesnake bite to his arm.

"Apparently the snake spooked the horse, Loren fell off, and the snake got him." Al said, "Most of these bites are dry, except when there's young nearby. There's probably a nest around here, we best be going."

"We'll pick him up on our way back. It looks like the other guys tried to help him, so they may not be that far ahead."

About two hundred miles southeast of the New Mexico border, John and Al caught up to them, as they stopped to give their horses a short respite. The outlaws saw the law men coming, and began firing on them. John and Al dismounted and got behind some brush off to the side. The two men mounted their horses. John and Al pulled their weapons and began shooting. Both horses were hit, and went down. The men again pulled their weapons. John and Al responded, killing one of the men, the other threw his hands in the air.

The Marshals threw the dead man back in the bushes for the next stage, or the buzzards, whichever came first. Al went over and shot both horses, as they had been mortally wounded. He got no enjoyment out of that part of his job. He and John were able to pull them off the road.

Al tied Loren's brother over the horse. John realized the three would have to take it easy going back. They stopped at a nearby farm, where John bought a horse and saddle. He pulled the outlaw off Al's horse put him on the one they just purchased, tying his hands to the saddle horn. The sun went down as the three reached Tucson. The trip back in had been cold and dusty. A sandstorm blew up as they arrived. John took the prisoner to the jail and put him in a cell before he and Al headed for home. Brett had already called Jack in to replace him for the night.

Just After cleaning up, John came into the house. He looked forward to a good meal having had nothing to eat except a light breakfast and hardtack that day. Barbara didn't disappoint him. She figured her husband would be hungry and fixed him a dinner of roast pheasant with all the trimmings. Before dinner he went in to get a glimpse of his daughter lying in her crib sleeping, her toy bear nestled against her cheek. John went out to the dining room where he and Barbara enjoyed the meal and afterward pleasant conversation on the couch.

"Jack came by this morning and told me what happened at the jail last night. I really wasn't sure whether you'd get back tonight or not, but I'm glad you did."

"Sam was a good friend and I'll miss his tall tales," John said. "I imagine they'll probably have a funeral service for him Sunday."

"Jack told me he would go to see Penelope and tell her about her husband," Barbara said. "That's one job I could never get used to."

After dinner the two went into the den and talked in front of a warm fire. Afterwards they went to bed where they started to make love. Ellie started crying and Barbara had to go in the other room. John lay there a bit frustrated until she returned.

The next morning John got up and went to the office. The circuit judge came in that morning and the marshal got the prisoner ready for the courtroom. Al brought down the buckboard after Brett got in the office. John and Al took the outlaw out in handcuffs, and unceremoniously threw him on the back of the wagon. They were hauled down to the courthouse where court deputies took him into the room at the end of the hall where they processed him, and then into the courtroom. A couple minutes later the judge came in. "You're charged with the murder of a peace officer and another prisoner while in custody. What's your plea?"

Frank spoke up. "My younger brother, Loren killed the peace officer and the prisoner. Neither of us had anything to do with it."

"You're also charged with the robbery and murder of three men on the stage. Are you going to blame your brother for that to?" The judge said. "Unfortunately the snake that killed your brother isn't here to stand trial, so I guess you'll have to eat that one too."

John guessed the man hadn't remembered the stagecoach when he came up with his story. He saw the smug look on the face of the man before the judge sentenced him to hang the next morning. They cuffed the prisoner and took him out to the wagon and back to the jail.

A little later, Barbara and Ellie came to the jail with lunches for the men. Frankie brought in lunch for the prisoner and took it back. He came back out as Barbara served potato salad and sandwiches to the deputies. After lunch, the Marshal escorted his wife back out to the buggy.

"I just cleaned up the buggy a couple days ago," John said. "Looks like you went through a sandstorm again."

"It started coming up just as I left the farm," Barbara said. It cleared up just before we got here, but it looks like it's blowing this way."

They saw it coming from the end of the street, and the marshal took his wife back inside the jail until it blew over. The deputies remained inside as well. About an hour later it cleared out. When John and Barbara and their daughter went back outside, sand had covered everything. Fred came out with the broom and swept the boardwalk in front of the jail. Proprietors of other stores did the same. After helping his wife on the buggy, John watched as she turned the buggy around and headed back home.

Fred and the other deputies started doing their rounds. John went inside to check on his prisoners. Both asked John to send word to their families in Albuquerque, New Mexico. The Marshal agreed and sent a message by stage that afternoon. There were few problems the rest of the day and Al had taken care of both of them. One had been a bar fight, the other a dispute at the general store.

The Marshal left early that afternoon leaving Hank in charge for the night. Getting back to the farm, John put up the horse and went to the pump for water to clean the buggy. He then went back to the well pump and cleaned himself up. Going back to the house, he noticed Barbara had already swept the porch and cleaned things up outside. John went inside to a good meal and then spent time with his wife in the living room before going to bed.

The Marshal got out early the next morning after a cup of coffee and hardtack. He let Barbara sleep in. Being cold outside, he wore a warm jacket. He saddled the horse and went to town. John went to the stable boarded the horse, went to the office and relieved Hank.

"I just took the prisoners some coffee from across the street," Hank said. "I just don't understand it, the dead look those guys have in their eyes, like they just don't care about anything or anybody."

"That's the reason they're in here, Hank. Letting them out, they would probably do the same, or worse. It was nice of you to take them coffee. Now we have to get them cuffed and back to the courtyard.

A large audience had assembled there, including the families of those killed. The two men were both taken up the stairs, fighting every step of the way. They were given last rites by a minister before hoods were put over their heads. The spectacle ended in minutes as the two dropped to their death.

Both bodies were taken off the hangman's ropes, carried over to the undertaker's wagon and hauled off for burial. John and Al returned to the office. Brett and Hank came out to witness the spectacle as well, and went back to the jail with them.

Barbara had just showed up with lunch when the four walked in the door. She handed Ellie to John, while she put out the lunch.

"Judging from the crowd outside, I'd say those two were hung. John, you know I don't like it, but if it were you instead of Sam, I'd want the same."

Al looked at John, "if I had it my way, I would have shot them both on the trail and laid them on top of Loren."

"I know how you feel, Al," John said. "This whole thing of Loren doing what he did didn't make a lot of sense, but I guess you have to think about what you'd do in a similar situation."

Barbara took Ellie back to the jail where she nursed her daughter, while the men had lunch. Lunch didn't go down easy after what they had witnessed that morning, especially considering Loren had been a friend to all of them.

After lunch, Al and Brett went out on patrol, and Hank headed home. John helped his wife and daughter onto the buggy and watched as it disappeared down the street. Being warm outside, he sat on the bench in front of the jail with his feet on the hitching rail. Sam's family came over to thank John.

"John," Sam's uncle said, "I just want you to know how much we appreciate what you did. I don't think I could've slept another night if those two had gotten away."

"You know, Jacob, I feel the same way. Sam was one of my deputies, and also a close friend. Frankly, I wouldn't have returned without them, either dead or alive. Please let me know when services will be held for him. I know they'll have something at the church for him this Sunday."

Jacob and his family left in the buggy as John watched. He knew he could never get used to this, and he hoped he never would. He sat down again, with his feet up. The next couple hours remained reasonably quiet. As usual, Al brought in a man who had gotten drunk up the street, and started waving his gun around. After putting the man in jail, Al came out and sat with John.

"Sam's family came by," John said. "They'll have a service on Sunday. It's possible the funeral and burial will be the same day. I'm sure we'll all miss the guy."

After a while, Al got up and went back on patrol. Brett had been off, checking some of the other saloons that afternoon. John heard shots fired down the street. He went inside and got his gun and holster off the hook and headed down to where the noise had come from. Going down the sidewalk, he saw three men coming toward him in a cloud of dust at full gallop. One of the men, seeing John took a shot, hitting him on the left shoulder. John went down on the boardwalk, turned shooting and killing one of the men off his horse. The other two continued out of town.

Brett came down the sidewalk toward the stable and saw his boss lying there, bleeding. Al had been winged, but being on horseback, picked up John, and took him to the doc's office above the stable. The doctor had a look at Al, and found him to be okay. A bullet had just grazed his shoulder. The two men carried John into the back room.

   Brett waited outside while the doctor checked on Al. When he came out, the two stopped at Jack's place, and told him what happened. Jack got on his horse and immediately Brett sent him back to take care of the office while they were gone. Jack didn't like it, but realized of the two, Al would more likely be able to   follow a trail.

   The two men took off going south, then east. The tracks turned off toward Tombstone, but stopped outside of Bisbee, at the Copper Queen. Brett and Al looked at each other, and shook their heads. Hoping he wouldn't be recognized, Brett walked in, leaving Al in front of the doors. He saw the man sitting at the gaming table. He carefully looked around and didn't see the other. Brett immediately walked over to the gaming table, and put the man in cuffs. Al came in when he saw Brett do this. The bartender said the man's partner had gone upstairs with one of the girls. Being no sheriff close by, Brett handcuffed the prisoner to the hitching-post outside.

   Getting his partner's room number out of the man, the two made their way inside and up the stairs. He could hear screams from a woman in the room. Brett busted into the room and saw the outlaw going for his gun. Brett immediately shot and killed the man. The young woman panicked and ran down the stairs with very little on.

Brett had the man carried downstairs by a couple of the men in the bar. They tied him to his horse, and his partner, to his saddle horn. The men had been on a winning streak, and those winnings were given to the bartender, to pay for the damages. The three men headed back to Tucson, returning at dusk. The marshals took the outlaw to the jail and his partner to the undertaker.

The weather had turned nasty again with a strong, cold wind blowing. The two peace officers walked up the stairway into the doc's office.

"How's John doing?" Brett said.

"I sent word for Barbara to bring the buggy down to pick him up in a few hours. He's sleeping right now and he'll stay that way until the laudanum wears off."

"When he wakes up, tell him we can handle the office for a few days or longer if he needs it. According to Jack, things are quiet right now."

Brett and Al went back to the office leaving Jack in charge for the night. Jack went back and briefly talked to the prisoner. The man sat on the edge of the cot with his head in his hands.

He looked up at Brett. "The guy you killed was my brother, you know. How did you know where to find us?"

"The guy that was with me is an Indian tracker. Your trail wasn't that hard to follow, Brett said. "I'm sorry about your brother, but it was self-defense."

"I guess I should've left him out of this," Bob said. "We were just trying to get a fresh start. We got in trouble a few years back and spent a few years in jail."

"Your brother was the only one killed, so you won't hang, however you will do time. The judge will be here in the morning."

Jack felt sorry for the guy, but he also felt sorry for John, who almost got himself killed. He sat down behind John's desk for the night. Brett and Al stopped at the saloon for a drink. It'd been a long day. The weather remained cold and windy, blowing a fair amount of sand.

Barbara decided to leave John at the Doc's place overnight, and pick him up in the morning. She nursed Ellie, put her down and went to bed. She had a restless sleep that night with dreams of John being shot, and having to attend his funeral.

The next morning she awoke, dressed herself and Ellie. She nursed Ellie and went into the kitchen to get a bite. Afterward Barbara hitched a horse to the buggy and dressed herself and

Ellie warmly, then left for town. She rode to the doc's office, and carried her daughter up the stairway.

"How's my husband doing?" Barbara said. "I guess he'll be hurting for a few days."

"Yes, he will. He tried to get up this morning to go back to work. He got only about halfway off the bed. He'll be tired for a few days. In the meantime give him a spoonful of this when the pain gets bad," he said, handing her a bottle.

The two carefully helped John down the stairway into the waiting buggy. Barbara went back upstairs and brought her daughter down, putting her on her father's lap. After thanking the doctor, the three rode off for home.

On getting there, Barbara took her daughter to her crib and then helped her husband into the house and to bed. She went outside, put up the horse and buggy, and returned to the house. She went into the bedroom and sat on the bed next to her husband.

"How are you feeling, honey?" Barbara said. "The doc gave me a bottle of laudanum in case you need it. He told me that stuff is easy to get addicted to, so to be careful."

"The whole thing happened so fast. I saw the three coming from the bank, with masks on. I yelled at them to stop, one took a shot at me, and I returned fire on my way down. That's about all I remember."

"I guess the doc told you, the man you shot off the horse is dead. **Al** and Brett went to a hotel near Bisbee, where they found the other two. Brett had to kill one of them, and brought the dead man and his partner back. He's looking to go to court this morning."

About that time, she heard her husband snoring lightly, and left the room to check on their daughter.

The next morning, Brett took his prisoner to the courtroom along with the man who got drunk and started shooting up the town. They were both taken down and turned over to the deputies at the courthouse. Al and Brett were there to testify. The man who got drunk came first. The judge came in.

"Barney, I don't know how many times I have to tell you, if you're going to drink, leave the gun at home. This time the deputy's not going to give it back to you. On top of that you'll spend the next six months in jail. Next time your sentence will be figured in years instead of months." Barney looked shocked.

A deputy came in and took him outside of the room in handcuffs. The other man came before the judge.

"The only thing I have to say to you is, it's a good thing our marshal wasn't killed, or I'd go pull the rope myself. I guess the last five years the judge in Phoenix gave you wasn't enough. This time we'll try ten. I'm giving you fair warning, I better never see you in my courtroom again." His gavel hit the table.

The deputies took the man to the stagecoach. The man charged with drunkenness went to Prescott to the prison there. The coach took the man that shot John to the train station, where he would be transported to Yuma Territorial Prison.

After getting their prisoner secured, Al and Brett returned to the office. The men relieved Jack when they got there. Les came in to help Al on his patrols. Brett sat back at John's desk and wondered how soon John would be back. He fixed a cup of coffee, and like John, enjoyed sitting outside. Being the weather warmed up, he found it pleasant.

That pleasantness didn't last long. He heard a shot coming from the general store down the street. Luckily he had his horse tied to the hitching-post in front of him, and immediately rode down to the general store.

Al came out of the store. "He went that way," Al said pointing west. He grabbed the horse belonging to the storekeeper, and with Brett, took off after the man.

"Is anybody hurt? "Brett said as the two rode off.

"The storekeeper's wife, she's dead. One of the men in the store said he would stay, until the doctor showed up, and that he saw the man riding off to the west."

"Did anybody get a look at the man?" Brett said. "I'm assuming it was a robbery?"

"I didn't have time to look. I just heard the shot, went in and saw Larry kneeling over Janice's dead body."

"Dammit, why did it have to be Janice?" Brett said. "She's just too nice a person. I'll want to see that bastard hang, if I don't kill him first."

The man's trail headed west and then south toward Mexico. The deputies took off after him at full gallop. Within a couple of hours, they caught up to the man, who had stopped to rest his horse off the trail. They almost missed him, but were able to stop before he saw them. They got off their horses and slowly and quietly made their way to the man. He started to mount his horse when the two deputies yelled at him. He made the mistake of drawing his gun. Brett shot the man in the heart, killing him instantly.

The deputies tied the man over his horse, and headed back to town, as periods of dust came up. Many of the townspeople stood outside the store in shock. They began to applaud as the deputies passed them on the way to the undertaker. They left the body off, and took the three horses to the stable where they would be fed and watered. The outlaw's horse would be given to the Marshal's office. The two deputies returned to the office. Brett filled out the necessary paperwork and Al went back to his rounds. Jack returned home after putting in a lot of hours in the office.

Les came down to spend the night taking care of the jail. Brett and Al headed home after a quick beer at Jake's. Both were tired from the day's activities.

Barbara took their daughter to her father. He woke up when he heard them come in the room. He took Ellie from her mother and lightly bounced her up and down on his stomach.

"I think you're feeding our daughter a little too well. She starting to feel a little heavy," John said. "I wonder how the guys are getting along in town."

"That's nothing for you to worry about right now. I have a lot of respect for your judgment," Barbara said. "You chose Brett to fill in for you when you're gone, and I think he's probably doing a good job of it."

"I guess you're right," John said. "Here, take Ellie. She is getting a little heavy for me, and I can feel that laudanum starting to take effect again."

Barbara took the child back to her room and after nursing her, laid her down in her crib with her toy bear. She came out to the kitchen to fix a bite for her and her husband. She held off taking John's meal to him until he woke up. She had slowly been weeding him off the drug, and figured he'd be normal in a day or two.

The next morning John felt more awake than usual. He realized with his arm the way it hurt him, he would still be in no condition to work. He wanted to go to town, but Barbara put her foot down on that one. She knew he needed the rest, because the doctor had told her he would have to recover before going back.

Everything stayed quiet when Brett got to the office that morning. He relieved Les, who soon left the office and headed home. Both Jack and Al got there minutes later. The three had coffee together before the deputies went out on patrol. Brett had a few reports to write up before going out. Later, he went back to check on the jail. With everything in order, and the cells empty, Brett went back to his desk. Getting a little bored, he strapped on his gun belt and walked over to the saloon across the street. He heard the piano playing.

"Hi, Jake, sounds like things are nice and quiet in here, just the way I like it."

"That goes double for me. I saw a couple guys in here earlier. I don't know why, but they just looked like trouble. They were on the other side of the room, so I couldn't make out anything. They may have been with a cattle drive, I just don't k now. I'll let you know if they cause any trouble."

With that, Brett left the saloon and went back to the office, where he sat outside, and enjoyed the weather. His respite didn't last long. About a half hour later he heard gunfire coming from down the street. He mounted his horse and headed towards where he heard the shots. They came from the bank several blocks down the street. His deputies were not at the scene. He pulled his gun and went into the front door of the bank. The bank guard lay bleeding on the floor. A man stood over him trying to help. He turned to Brett.

"There were two of them Marshal. They lit out the back door. There wasn't any reason for them to shoot Bill. I managed to get the bleeding stopped and I'll get somebody to help me get him down to docs."

"Did you recognize either of them, or can you give me a description?"

"No, they were both wearing bandannas over their face. The one man had a slight limp, that's about all I can tell you. They both had on blue jeans, and checkered, long-sleeved shirts."

Brett faced the other three customers. "Did any of you see which way they went?"

"I think they took off heading west," one of the men said. "At least that's what it sounded like. They said something about heading to Tombstone, but I think they were trying to throw you off their trail by saying that."

About that time, Al showed up at the bank. He went out, checked the tracks, and verified what the customer had said. He and Brett mounted up and took off West at full gallop. The bank customer hit it right. The two were heading for Mexico. Al and Brett caught up to them in about an hour. The outlaw's horses had given out and needed water and rest. The deputy's horses were in much better condition.

The men drew their pistols and started firing. Fortunately the deputies were out of range. Brett took his rifle, and shot one of the men in the leg, telling the other to drop his weapon. Wisely, the man did as Brett told him. Al drew his pistol and rode up to the men while Brett kept them covered.

"Turn around and face the tree," Al said. Don't try anything funny and you won't get hurt."

By that time Brett had the other man handcuffed and in custody. He took the man's bandanna and wrapped it around his leg, above the wound. He had lost a lot of blood. Brett wasn't sure whether or not the man would make it back to town. Al started a fire heating up his knife. He pulled the bullet out of the outlaw's leg, after giving the man a piece of bark to bite down on.

Al and Brett took the men to a small town about a mile off the trail. The doctor, more of a horse doctor, did what he could. He managed to get the bleeding stopped, and the marshals tied their prisoner on a horse. They took the two men back to the jail in Tucson.

Being late in the evening when they got back, Jack relieved Al after he and Brett had taken the wounded man to the doc's office.

"How's Bill doing, did he make it?"

"I almost lost him, but I think he'll make it," Doc said. "He's in the other room, pretty doped up, and sleeping.

Brett went back to the office after taking his horse to the stable to be rubbed down and fed.

"I have some paperwork to get caught up on in case the circuit Judge shows up in the morning," Brett said. "You might go down to the doc's office and bring the prisoner back when docs done patching him up."

A couple of hours later Jack brought the prisoner back into the office. He took the outlaw back to the jail and put him in a cell next to his partner.

"The two of you better hope that Bill pulls through this. He's a friend of the circuit Judge, and if anything happens to him, you'll both hang."

"Marshal, I need something to drink to kill the pain so I can sleep."

"You can stay awake all night. Maybe that will give you a chance to think about what you did."

Jack went back into the office. "Those guys are both secure, Brett. Why don't you take off and go on home, I'll handle things from here out."

"That sounds like a good idea, Jack," Brett said. "I'll grab a drink at Jake's, and head home."

Brett walked down the street to the saloon and up to the bar.

"How's it going, Jake?" Brett said. "You hit it right with those two clowns. They were up to no good."

"Oh, how's that Brett?" Jake said. "What did they do?"

"Well, they held up the bank down the street, shot Bill Freeman, and led me and Al on a chase practically to the border. We just got back a couple of hours ago."

"God, Brett, how's Bill doing?"

"He's resting over at docs place right now. Doc says he'll probably make it."

"Well, that's good," Jake said. "What'll you have, the usual?"

"Yeah, just a beer, I never could get into the strong stuff."

About a half hour later, Brett walked out of the saloon and down to the stable to pick up his horse and head for home. It had been a long day, and it wore him out.

The next morning John came into the office. His shoulder still remained in a sling. Jack sat and talked with the prisoners. John walked back and saw the two men in jail.

"Good morning Jack," John said. "Everything okay this morning?"

"It is now," Jack said. "Brett and Al chased these two practically to the Mexican border. They held up the bank down the street and shot Bill Freeman yesterday."

"Bill Freeman? Is he okay?"

"I hope so, and these two better hope so too."

"Why don't you go on home, Jack? I can take it from here."

"Aren't you supposed to be taking it easy, John?"

"Yeah, well, you know, there's only so long you can do that."

"Does Barbara know you're here?"

"I imagine she's probably figured it out by now. I left before she woke up."

"Well, it's your funeral," Jack said, getting up to leave the office.

John went out and sat at his desk. He picked up the arrest report from the night before, and began going through it. Brett came into the office.

"Well, hello John," Brett said. "I didn't expect to see you for a couple of days."

"Yeah, well I got tired of sitting around with nothing to do and being waited on hand and foot. Women seem to enjoy that sort of thing for some reason."

"Well you better take it easy. I can handle any heavy stuff that comes in. You just keep the chair warm."

Al came into the office. He had just come from the county courthouse.

"Judge Riley is here from Prescott. He told me to get the prisoners down to his Courthouse this morning. I guess this is the third time they've been in trouble."

Brett walked down to the stable for a buckboard while Al got the prisoners ready for transport. After cuffing them, he took them outside, where he and Brett put them on the back of the wagon. They took the prisoners to the courthouse for trial. Getting there, Al helped the marshals get the prisoners into the court of law, while Brett handed the paperwork to the judge.

"Al said you wanted to try these guys personally." Brett said. "I take it you've had run-ins with them before?"

"More than once," Judge Riley said. "They got away with a payroll up near Prescott. The stage driver was shot, and almost killed. They were sentenced to twenty years in prison. I don't understand why they're out."

"If they escaped from Yuma, we should've heard about it," Brett said.

"Well, if they did, they'll get another chance."

The two men were brought into the courtroom. Fear came over their faces as they recognized the presiding judge.

"Well, if it isn't the Larson brothers. I know better than to think anybody let you out, so I'm assuming you just recently escaped. I wish I had the authority to hang you both, but about all I can do is send you back to Yuma. This time any type of parole will be out of the question. You're looking at life now."

The two men were cuffed, led out of the courtroom, and out to the wagon in front. Al and Brett took them to the train station, and waited for the train to come before taking them off the wagon. It arrived a half hour later, and Brett accompanied the two outlaws to Yuma.

Al returned to the office and told John that Brett would be gone a couple of days. John called in a couple of deputies to take his place. About noon, Barbara and their daughter showed up with lunches for the men. She wasn't in a very good mood she walked into the office and placed the basket on the table.

"What's this all about?" She said. "You know the doctor told you to stay quiet!"

"I'm taking it very easy. I've been delegating authority all morning. Come on honey, you know I can't just lie around."

"You know what will happen if that wound on your shoulder opens up. The doc said you could lose the use of it."

"I'm being very careful. I've got the sling tightened up. Besides, the wound is healing nicely."

Barbara shook her head. "Well, don't blame me if something happens to it."

Barbara set out the lunch for John and his deputies. John made it a point to admire Ellie and use his left arm to play with her.

"Where's Brett?" Barbara said. "He's usually the first one here."

"He's transporting a couple of prisoners to Yuma. He won't be back until the day after tomorrow."

The deputies just started enjoying their lunch when a man ran into the office.

"Marshal, there's trouble over at Jake's. A couple of gamblers got into it. One man's been stabbed. The guy started threatening one of the other players, and Jake came up from behind the bar and hit the man in the head with a beer bottle and knocked him out."

"Well it sounds like Jake has the situation well in hand," John said. "Did anybody get the doc?"

"Yeah, he sent one of the other guys up there, told me to come get you."

"That doesn't sound like anything too dangerous. You guys enjoy lunch. I'll go see what Jake wants."

John accompanied the man to the saloon up the street. The doctor pulled the guys shirt off, when John got there. The chest wound bled profusely as the doctor tried to stop it. The man lying on the floor tried to get up, but Jake pushed him down again.

"Oh, hi John," Jake said. "Stan here accused the guy of cheating and decided to do something about it. I tried to stop it, but I couldn't. He began to turn on one of the other men at the table, so I hit him with the beer bottle."

Chapter 5

"It looks like Stan may have been justified," Doc said. "This guy had several cards up his sleeve."

"I thought he seemed to be doing awfully well for a guy that claimed he didn't know how to gamble," Barney Wellman said. "Stan saw something, got mad and stood up pulling his knife."

Thinking John may need help, Al walked into the saloon. He took Stan into custody and walked him across the street to the jail. Doc got a couple guys in the saloon to carry the card cheat up to his office. He hadn't died, but Doc didn't hold out much hope for him.

John and Al returned to the office. Al sat at John's desk and wrote up the reports for John, knowing his arm still hurt from the gunshot. John sat on the chair in the corner, and went through the reports after Al had finished them. Jack showed up shortly after. Al and John crossed the street to Jake's saloon and got a couple of beers.

"How's Stan doing?" Jake said. "Ralph, the other guy at the table that Stan began to turn on, turned out to be wanted in Phoenix as well as George Fremont, the victim."

"Stan's got a hell of a headache, but he'll be okay. If Fremont dies, Stan could be charged with involuntary manslaughter, but I think that's about as far as a judge would take it."

"I had Gene pick up Ralph Jacobs as he started to get on the stage coach," John said. "I've got him locked up as well. I think I'll let the circuit judge sort it out."

About an hour later, John and Al went down to the stable. Their horses were saddled and ready to go. Both John and Al headed for home. Barbara put dinner on the table when she saw her husband come through the gates and into the barn. The horse had already been fed and watered. John went to the pump and cleaned up a little before going into the house.

"How's my girl tonight," John said, kissing the back of her neck. "Let me run back, see Ellie, and I'll come right back."

John could tell his wife had not gotten over being mad at him. He realized she just worried about him. He had tried to explain to her earlier why he felt he needed to go back to work, but he didn't think she listened to what he said.

John came up from the bedroom to the dining room table. He gave his wife a wide smile. "Something sure smells good."

"It's not going to work!" Barbara said. "You know the doc told you to stay in bed a couple more days. You don't want that arm becoming unusable, do you?"

"Of course not, the deputies did all the work for me, even filling out the paperwork. I just didn't feel right sitting here doing nothing."

After dinner, John went into the living room. The weather had warmed up so the fire wasn't necessary. After cleaning up in the kitchen, Barbara came in and sat with him. John put his arm around her, and didn't say anything. After a while they began a conversation which cleared the air. John promised her he wouldn't do any heavy work at his office in town. The two slept well that night.

The next morning John got up a little late and joined Barbara at the breakfast table. She had gone back and nursed Ellie before John woke up. After a breakfast of ham and eggs, John mounted up and rode into town. John noticed the weather had gotten a little warmer in the morning. He stabled his horse and walked down to the office where he found Jack snoozing at his desk.

"Those two behave themselves last night?" John said.

"I heard a few threats back there, but nothing that serious."

"Have you heard anything about George Fremont?"

"No, nothing yet, I can run up to the doc's office if you want?"

"That's all right. I'll run up there after I see the prisoners."

John walked back to the cells. Stan Larson lay back on his bunk. John could tell he got little sleep. Ralph Jacobs snored in the next cell.

"Is there any word on George Fremont?" Stan said. "I just had a little too much to drink last night. I don't know what came over me, but when I caught those two cheating, I guess I lost it."

"I can't say as I blame you, Stan. I'm going to run over to the Doc's. We found both he and Ralph Jacobs are wanted in Phoenix for cheating at cards as well. You know Stan; you really should've let me handle this."

John went out and walked down to Doc's. He went up the stairs and into the office. He could hear the doctor in the other room and walked in.

"Well I guess they won't bring Stan up on murder charges anyway," John said. "How's he doing Doc?"

"He'll be able to leave here, probably sometime toward the end of the week. He's been in and out of consciousness most of the night."

"Well, that's good news. I think I'm going to go ahead and release Stan on bail. His family is here, so I doubt he's going to try to go anywhere. On the other hand, I'll send Ralph Jacob back to Phoenix to stand trial there."

John walked back down to the Marshal's office. Jack had already left and Al sat at the desk.

"You can get Stan and bring him out here," John said "I'll fill out some paperwork."

Al pulled the keys from the desk drawer and walked back to the jail where he unlocked the cell that held Stan. The two men walked out to the front desk and sat down.

"You're a lucky man, Stan," John said. "George Fremont's going to be laid up at docs, but he should be up and around by the end of the week. I'll put him on the train to Prescott where he'll be tried for cheating at gambling, and anything else they can think of."

"Thank you John, I don't think I could've slept comfortably knowing I had killed somebody."

After posting bail, Stan walked out of the office and over to the saloon. Jake apologized to him for the incident with the beer bottle. Stan thanked him for saving him from a possible murder rap.

Late that afternoon Brett returned from Yuma by train. John had a horse and buggy sent to the train station to pick him up and bring him back to the Marshal's office. As he got back, a horse came at full gallop from a couple of miles away. Brett saw the dust of the horse at full gallop coming up the street. The rider came directly to the Marshal's office and up to Brett as he got off of the buggy.

"Marshal there's been a hold-up at the essay office down on Pennington Street. Lou Major has been shot. A couple guys are bringing him down to the docs now."

Brett took the man into the office where John sat behind his desk. The man repeated to John what he had told Brett. John rode with Brett on the buggy down to the livery stable where the two men got their horses. They rode to the assay office at full gallop. Deputy Fred Warren had gotten there minutes before and took down statements from a couple of the other agents in the office. They gave John a pretty good description of the three men who all wore bandanna masks.

John sent Fred along with three other deputies who took care of that part of town, to chase down the bandits. Al had already been called to come down, and joined the four deputies in pursuit of the outlaws.

"Okay Carl, what happened here?" John said. "Was Lou the only one injured?"

"Lou got careless and tried to stop them. Brandon had warned all of us in case of a robbery like this, to just give the outlaws what they wanted and try to get as good a description as possible of them and their horses."

"How badly was Lou injured?" John said. "Was he able to talk?"

"He talked to Fred, and gave him a statement before he passed out. A couple of the boys from across the street took him to the docs down by your office."

After getting all the information he could, John rode back to the Marshal's office where deputy marshal Leo Wilson had been called in by Al to watch the office. John lashed his horse to the hitching-rail in front. As it got late in the afternoon, John would be heading for home as soon as he filled out the reports on the incident.

"I just heard from Doc. Lou Peterson will probably make it," Leo Wilson said. "He took a bullet to the neck, just barely grazing a blood vessel there. Doc was able to patch it up. Did anyone say how much they made off with?"

"They got close to $20,000 in gold and cash. It was supposed to be taken by train to Phoenix in the morning. With that much gold they probably took it by buckboard," John said. "Even with their head start, Al should be able to track them before they get too far."

"I called in Ben and Jared for patrol tonight," Leo said. "Everything seems to have calmed down now."

"I'm going to run over to Jake's for couple minutes to see if anybody heard anything about the robbery. I'll be taking off for home after that. Have a good one."

John went up the street to Jake's. A couple of cowboys at the bar heard shots coming into town, but didn't pay much attention to them. Nobody saw anything. John went back and got his horse from the hitching rail and headed back to his farm. Barbara brought Ellie out onto the porch when she saw John ride up. He put his horse up, cleaned up at the pump, and walked over to greet his family at the front door.

He took Ellie from Barbara and carried her back to her bedroom. Barbara had nursed her before John got home, making her sleepy. After putting her down, John walked out to the kitchen, and gave his wife a long kiss and hug.

"Anything exciting happen in town since I left," Barbara said. "It seemed pretty quiet."

"Unfortunately, it didn't stay that way. There was a robbery at the assay office over on Pennington Street. I've got Al, and four deputies, out on the trail going after them now."

"Well I'm glad you didn't go out with them. How's your arm doing?"

"Oh, pretty well considering. Most of my day's been behind the desk, but I did have to get out when we got the call from the assay office."

The two enjoyed a quiet dinner before retiring to the den. There they spent about an hour in conversation, while Barbara changed the dressing on his arm. They got to bed early that night and enjoyed each other's company for a while, before turning over for the night.

The next morning, after breakfast and coffee, John went to the barn, saddled up, and rode into town. Getting to the office he found Leo in the back talking to two new prisoners that had been brought in during the night.

John walked in. "Good morning Leo, it looks like you had a busy night."

"These are two of the guys involved. The other three have been strapped to their saddles, and taken to the undertaker," Leo said. "I've tried to get information out of them, but they clammed up."

"Was the gold recovered?"

"Yes, they found all of it. There's still several hundred dollars in cash missing, and they're not saying where it went."

"Well maybe they'll loosen up if they realize they'll be dangling from a noose tomorrow morning."

"What do you mean, Marshal," one of the men said. "You can't hang us just for stealing."

John winked at Leo. "Who said anything about stealing? This will be for murder in the commission of a robbery, and don't try that old one about telling us the other guys did it, because that won't fly."

"Honest Marshal, we just winged him."

"Tell that to his widow. You tell the truth about how this whole thing went down and where the rest of the money is, and the judge might spare the noose."

John and Leo walked out into the office, giving the criminals time to think about it. It didn't take long. They were given the location of a man supplying them with the necessary provisions. They paid him for his silence. His place of business is a dry goods store on Congress Street. That morning the Marshal's recovered the rest of the money and returned it to the essay office. The store owner, Wilhelm Grey went to jail.

"Marshal, you told us if you recovered the money, we wouldn't swing, is that true?" One of the outlaws said.

"Yes, I'll put in a good word with the judge and see to it that you don't hang," the Marshal said. "I need to get a statement from you about your arrest. I'll do that after lunch this afternoon."

At about noon that morning, Barbara brought Ellie and the lunches in for her husband and his deputies. A few minutes later Bobby, who worked in the café across the street, brought in lunches for the two incarcerated outlaws. He took them back, and came out a few minutes later.

"Will those guys need dinner tonight?" He said. "Frank told me to ask you."

"Yes, and probably breakfast tomorrow morning. I don't know what time the judge will be getting here."

"Okay, I'll let him know." Bobby left the office.

Barbara finished unpacking the lunches from the basket. She had fixed roast beef sandwiches on homemade bread. John spent that time bouncing Ellie on his knee. After finishing lunch John escorted Barbara and his daughter outside to the buggy, and watched as they disappeared down the street. At times like this he felt like the luckiest man in the world. The deputies returned to their rounds throughout the city.

John went back inside to check on his prisoners before going out to the bench in front of the office. Being that his arm still hurt him, he decided to continue taking it a little easy. He figured if anything needed to be done, he had men that could do it. He dozed off in the afternoon sun.

About a half hour later shots ringing out from Jake's saloon woke him. He went inside the office and pulled one of his guns off the hook, leaving the holster behind. He ran up the street and met a man wearing a large sombrero coming out the batwing doors of the saloon. He took a shot in the air, stopping the man in his tracks.

"Okay, that's far enough. Slowly unbuckle your gun belt and drop it on the boardwalk."

A man came running out of the saloon and over to the Marshal. A look of relief came over him when he saw John had the man in custody.

"Okay Lester, what went on in there?"

"This guy came down the stairs," Lester said. "I think he was up there with one of the girls. One of the guys at the bar saw him, and pulled his gun out. This man drew and fired his gun hitting the guy in the chest."

"I was just going to get the doc when I saw you out here," Lester said. "I better get over there." He said, running down the street.

John handcuffed his prisoner to the hitching-rail in front of the saloon. He went inside to find a man bleeding on the floor in front of the bar, and Jake kneeling down over him. Still alive, the man clutched his chest in pain. Shortly afterward, the doctor came running into the bar and knelt down in front of the wounded man. After the doc put a bandage on the wound, two men carried him across the street and up the stairs to the doctor's office.

The Marshal un-cuffed his prisoner and took him into custody. Noticing his arm in a sling, the man took a swing at John. The marshal ducked before the man's fist hit him. The man didn't duck in time, and wound up on the ground. The marshal picked the guy up and walked him across the street and put him in jail. After getting himself a cup of coffee, John went into the jail and sat down across from the man.

"I don't think I've seen you around here before, what's your name?" The Marshal said. "Why did the guy try to shoot you? And please don't tell me you don't know."

"I broke it off with his sister a couple of weeks ago. I guess he didn't take too kindly to it."

"That's hardly anything to shoot a man over. If your story checks out, I may let you out this afternoon. I'm going to let your attempted attack on me go for now."

Al stayed in the office while the marshal went to check on the condition of the man at the doc's office.

"How's he doing doc?" John said. "It sounds like a family dispute, but somehow I'm not sure my prisoners telling the truth."

"He's probably not. I found this badge in the man's pocket. It looks like he's a deputy sheriff over near Prescott. He's going to be sore for a few days, but he'll live."

John went back over to his office. He walked back to the jail and sat down outside the cell.

"Why's he chasing you?" John said. "And don't lie to me anymore."

"I don't know what you're talking about Marshal. I've never seen him before this afternoon."

"Well, unfortunately for you, the guys carrying a badge," John said. "I'm going to ask you this one more time. Why's he after you?"

"I don't know, ask him."

"Have it your way. You better hope he pulls through."

John walked out to his desk and sat down. He would find out more of what this is about as soon as the man at the doc's office recovered from the gunshot.

Brett came into the office. He saw the prisoner in the jail through the open door.

"Who's that?" Brett said, sitting down. "Did he have anything to do with the shooting across the street earlier?"

"Yeah, it looks like a deputy sheriff from Prescott was after him. I won't know much until the deputy regains consciousness. That should happen a little later this afternoon."

The deputy from Prescott did regain consciousness that afternoon, but fell back into unconsciousness before the marshal had a chance to question him. Being late afternoon, John decided he'd had enough for one day. He would be back first thing in the morning to question the doctor's patient.

John went back to the office to let Brett know the deputy would probably not regain consciousness to the point where he could be lucid until the next morning.

"The other deputies haven't gotten here yet, but Jack should be getting back pretty soon," Brett said. "I can handle things until they get here. Why don't you call it a day?"

"That sounds like a good idea. Is our prisoner okay?"

"I think you made him a little nervous earlier. I couldn't get much out of him, but apparently he was just going through Prescott."

"Like I said many times before, you can't put a lot of credence in what most prisoners say," John said. "Well, if you've got everything covered here I think I'll head for home."

The Marshal walked down to the stables and picked up his horse. He had been fed and watered. The stable hand saddled him for John. He rode off toward his farm. Getting back, he didn't see the buggy in the barn. After cleaning up at the pump he went into the house. Barbara and Ellie were not there. He found this strange, but went in, got a cup of coffee, and went into the living room.

After a couple of hours he began getting nervous. He saddled his horse and rode back into town. He saw their buggy at the side of the doctor's office, and hurriedly went upstairs. Barbara sat on the sofa in tears when John came in. As he walked over and sat next to her, the doctor came out from the other room. He saw John sitting next to his wife, and came over to them.

"I'm sorry, John, I did everything I could for Ellie."

John looked at Barbara. He couldn't believe what he just heard. She broke down, and sobbed on John's shoulder. This news hadn't hit him yet, so he just looked at the doctor in disbelief.

"What's going on?" John said. "What happened to Ellie?"

"I don't really know, John," Doc Adams said. "Apparently she had a seizure at home, probably from a fall. There was nothing I could do for her."

"I heard a noise in her room after I nursed her," Barbara said in tears. "When I laid her in the crib, she started convulsing. She hit her head on the side of the crib reaching for her toy earlier, but certainly not hard enough to cause this."

"It wasn't your fault Barbara," the doc said. "It was just the way her head hit the crib that caused the problem. It ruptured a blood vessel."

John sat with his arm around Barbara, consoling her, for the next ten or fifteen minutes. He went into the other room to have a look at his daughter. He lifted her into his arms and started crying. He set her down, and went back to the outer office. He and Barbara returned to the farm. Neither he nor the doctor made any mention of the deputy's condition in the other room. John asked the doctor to talk to Brett in the morning.

Getting back, the two went into the house, and to the bedroom. Neither had any desire for food, but John gave them each a teaspoon of laudanum to help them sleep. Barbara cried her way to sleep in her husband's arms. John lay there listening to his wife's breathing and soon fell asleep himself.

The next morning John awoke and got up, letting his wife sleep. He realized she would need him there when she awoke. He went out to the kitchen and fixed coffee and got eggs ready to put on once Barbara awoke. He went outside to the barn and fed and watered the horses, giving them each an apple from the tree outside. He sat on a bale of hay inside the barn and began to sob uncontrollably. He realized the horrible pain that happened to him and Barbara the day before. He knew he had to be strong for her.

Returning to the house a little later, he found Barbara sitting at the dining room table with a cup of coffee. She had poured one for him as well.

"By instinct, I went to nurse Ellie this morning. John, she's gone. I just don't know how I'm going to go on."

"I'll ask one of the ladies from the church to come in and stay with you for a few days. I know I sound selfish, but I can't sit around here with nothing to do. I really have to work."

"I realize that," Barbara said. "I don't need anybody here with me."

"I don't need to go in today, in fact I don't think I can," John said. "I asked Doc Adams to let Brett know what happened yesterday and to go back to doc's office and question the deputy while he's there. He can handle it."

John went to the kitchen and fixed a breakfast of ham and eggs for him and his wife. Afterwards he took Barbara back to the bedroom and had her lie down while he cleaned up in the kitchen. Soon he came back into the bedroom. Barbara snored lightly as he came in. He decided to let her sleep and went out to the living room sofa. He had a hard time coming to terms with the loss of his little daughter.

Late that evening Barbara's medication wore off. She came out and heard her husband outside, doing chores. She fixed a nice dinner for him, before calling him in. The two discussed the possibility of another child. Both realized nobody could replace Ellie.

"We're not old enough for that to be a factor," John said. "I think having somebody around here for you to take care of would be a good idea."

"Probably so, but I don't think I could take another loss like that. We talked about a larger family before. Let's see how we feel a little later on."

The two went into the bedroom to get ready for a good night sleep. Luckily both slept well that night, after laudanum. The next morning Barbara got up and fixed breakfast for her husband. She encouraged him to go back to work."

"I'm going into town a little early this morning. I want to have a talk with a couple of the ladies from the church and arrange for services this Sunday. I'll bring lunches by for you and the deputies."

John rode into town that morning. He appreciated the clear weather and cool breeze. Not knowing what to expect, he rode his horse to the hitching-rail in front of the office, and went in. Al sat at the desk.

"Hello John," Al said. "I'm sure sorry to hear about Ellie. The wife and I want to pay our respects, so let me know when you plan to have the services for her."

"Thank you Al. She's making arrangements this morning with some of the women from the church. They'll probably hold the services this coming Sunday."

John went back to the jail, and found nobody there. He returned to the outer office.

"Where's our prisoner?" Marshal Green said. "I was just getting ready to walk down to doc's office."

"I put him on the train for Prescott yesterday afternoon. Doc said the deputy recovered enough to make the trip, so he took the prisoner with him."

Al left for home, and Brett showed up at the office. Five other deputies came in, and got their assignments for the day. All of them expressed their sorrow to John before they left. After a bit, John and Brett went out to the bench in front, putting their feet up. The town stayed quiet that morning. Jake walked over from his saloon.

"Good morning John, Brett," Jake said. "I, and it seems everybody else in town, is sure sorry about what happened to Ellie. The wife and I will be at her service. Do you know when it'll be?"

"Barbara is talking to some of the church people this morning. I should know something a little later. I'll be sure and let you know, thanks Jake."

Aside from a drunken brawl in a saloon across from the train depot, which one of his deputies took care of, things stayed pretty quiet for the rest of the morning. Barbara packed up a lunch for John and the deputies and brought it to the office shortly before three of the deputies showed up. The men all expressed their condolences to Barbara. She left for home after the men finished eating. John helped her onto the buggy.

"Are you okay, honey?" John said. "I can follow you home if you like."

"I'll be fine, don't worry about me. I'll see you this evening."

A domestic disturbance at a nearby farm interrupted the tranquility of the afternoon. John called Jack in to watch the office while he and Brett rode out to the farm. They went up to the front door, and yelled in.

"George, John Green, open up."

With no response and hearing a noise inside, the two marshals drew their guns and went in the house. George sat, tied to a chair, crying. Mattie, his wife, lay dead on the floor, with a gunshot to her chest.

"I didn't mean to do it," George said. "It was an accident."

"How the hell do you accidentally shoot somebody in the chest?" Brett said.

"John, you know both of us. We have a good marriage," George said. "I was cleaning the rifle, and I forgot to unload it."

Brett went over to the man and untied him. He looked at John, who motioned, "no". George fell to his knees on top of his wife, crying, as soon as Brett released his bonds. Knowing the man as a church deacon, and friend, John had no doubt he told the truth. After a few minutes, George talked to the marshals.

"Buddy, heard the gunshot and ran in here. He saw me holding the gun and tied me to the chair because I threatened to turn the gun on myself. He rode to town to get help. He was pretty badly shaken."

"We got word from the stable. I guess buddy went into the saloon, probably to get drunk."

Brett went over and put his hands on the man's shoulder. "I'll go hitch-up the buckboard. You can take Mattie to town on that."

After getting her loaded, George drove her to town, with the marshals following closely behind. The three pulled up in front of the doctor's office and a couple men from the stable came over and carried the body upstairs. Brett went back to the office to wait for the night deputy, and John took George over to Jake's.

"Hello George, I've been expecting you. I know you couldn't have hurt Mattie, unless completely by accident. How is she?"

The Marshal placed his hand on George's shoulder. "I'm afraid she didn't make it, Jake. I know George isn't a drinking man, but he definitely needs something to get rid of the pain."

John left him there and asked Jake to take George over to the jail and give him a bunk for the night after giving him a few drinks for the pain. He could leave for home in the morning. John went back to the office. Frank sat at the desk waiting for him.

"Brett told me what happened to George. I could never understand why things like that happen to good people. Your wife told Lilly that the services for your daughter will be Sunday. I was sure sorry to hear about her."

"Thank you, Frank. It's been quite a week. George is going to bunk over here for the night. You might go pick him up while he's still sober enough to walk. If you don't mind, I'd like to head for home. I'll see you in the morning."

John unhitched his horse from the rail in front, and rode off for home. Barbara stood on the porch as she saw him ride through the gate. After giving the horse a rubdown, a bucket of oats, and an Apple, he went to the pump, got cleaned up, and went to the porch to join his wife. After a long kiss, they went in the house.

Barbara had dinner on the stove, and got it ready while John went in the bedroom and changed. He came out to the dining room and sat down. The two said grace and a special prayer for their daughter. After dinner, and cleaning things up, they went into the den and sat together on the sofa. The marshal put his arm around his wife.

"Services for Ellie will be held day after tomorrow at the church," Barbara said. "Burial for her will be in the graveyard behind the church. God, John, I miss her so much."

"So do I, I looked forward to seeing her grow up into a beautiful young lady. I guess there must've been some reason for this, but I don't understand it."

Barbara began to cry on John's shoulder as he pulled her over to him. This weekend would be very hard on both of them. They sat there for the next couple of hours not saying much. Afterward, John pulled his wife to her feet, and led her into the bedroom. After getting ready for bed, John gave him and Barbara a spoon of laudanum, and held her in his arms until she fell asleep.

Late the next morning John got up and went to the kitchen where he fixed coffee and a breakfast of ham and eggs for him and his wife. John sat at the table, drinking coffee, when Barbara came out. There's no question she wasn't herself. After breakfast, she went back to the bedroom and to bed. John went out, saddled his horse, and rode into town. He left his horse at the stable and walked to his office. The Marshal came in to an empty office. He could hear talking in the back room. Frank listened as George talked about the life he and Mattie enjoyed over the years. They knew almost everybody in town.

"Good morning, Marshal," George said, seeing John at the door. "Frank and I were just reminiscing about our lives here in Tucson."

"I kind of know how you feel, George," John said. "Barbara and I spent a couple hours reminiscing about our daughter after I got in last night. Life plays dirty tricks on us sometimes."

George got off the bunk where he sat, and walked into the office. The Marshal walked him out to his buckboard that a stable hand brought down earlier.

"Thank you Marshal," George said. "I'll see you in church tomorrow."

"The wife told me they'll have services for Mattie tomorrow as well as Ellie," Frank said. "It's not going to be a happy day for anybody."

Al and a few deputies showed up that morning. They spread out to separate parts of town. Al went into the office and got coffee for him and John. They went out on the porch to enjoy the beautiful weather. Jake walked over from the saloon to check on George. The two had been friends for many years.

"Is George still here?" Jake said.

"No, he just left," the Marshal said. "It's going to take him some time to get over it. Frank says the services for George's wife will follow Ellie's at the church tomorrow."

"I don't know how the preachers going to handle that," Jake said. "From what I understand, between the two of them there probably won't be room in the church for everybody. I'll close the saloon down for the day, and be there."

Jake walked back across the street. Things stayed quiet for the next couple of hours. The stage came in from the Midwest, with seven passengers aboard. It stopped at the stable and the driver jumped down from his seat, and hurriedly came to the Marshal's office.

Chapter 6

"Is something wrong, Steve?" John said.

"There sure is. We were stopped some forty miles out of town. They made off with the strong box, and most of the valuables the passengers were carrying. Marshal, I recognized the leader, it was William Cantrell's nephew. Luckily, I guess I didn't show it."

"Cantrell, I haven't heard that name in a while." Was anybody hurt? John said.

"Only our pride, there were four outlaws with him. That strong box is pretty heavy. It was full of gold from the mines in Nevada. The passengers are pretty upset, but nobody was hurt."

About that time Brett showed up to take over for Frank who stayed on. Brett and the Marshal deputized several men in the saloon, and they quickly made their way to where the stage had been stopped. Al picked-up their trail. It looked like the men would probably be heading for Nogales.

The men rode long and hard, following Al to their quarry. By late afternoon Al spotted the outlaws. They had pulled off the road to rest and water their horses. As the deputies approached the men, the Marshal could tell they had been drinking. Not a smart thing to do under the circumstances, especially when they began to open fire on the deputies. The deputy marshals returned fire. Two of the deputies were mortally wounded. Cantrell and one of his men were the only outlaws to survive.

Although late in the afternoon, the men decided to ride back to Tucson, getting in late that evening. The marshals tied the three dead outlaws and two deputies to their horses for the return trip.

Getting back to Tucson, the marshal escorted Cantrell and the one surviving outlaw into the jail. The three other outlaws were taken to the undertaker for burial. He knew the law in Missouri hunted Cantrell, and the two outlaws would be sent back there by train the next day. The valuables belonging to the passengers were returned to their rightful owners. The strong box full of gold went into the bank for safekeeping.

"Did you feel the need to copy the behavior of your famous relative?" Brett said.

"I guess it just runs in the blood of our family," Cantrell said. "It beats dirt farming."

Brett looked through the bars at the man. "You can tell me all about that when you're swinging from a noose."

Brett and Al left Frank in charge of the prisoners and went up the street to join the Marshal and the other deputies at

Jake's place. Jake set up drinks for the Marshal and his deputies. Being late in the evening, the Marshal only had one beer before returning home. He got one of the horses from the stable and left his to be fed, watered, and given a rubdown.

Getting home that evening, John saw Barbara with a lantern, cleaning the buggy and getting it ready for the next day. John rode the horse into the barn. The horse had been fed and watered before leaving town. John pulled an apple from the tree and gave it to the animal.

Barbara came over to John and put her arm around him. The Marshal could tell his wife had been crying by the redness in her eyes. The two kissed and went into the house. Barbara had dinner ready in the oven, and turned up the heat when she came into the kitchen. The two sat at the table. John poured them each coffee as they waited for their meal to cook. After dinner and cleanup they went into the living room, and held each other. They soon went to bed.

The next morning Barbara removed the red bow from their daughters dress and replaced it with a black one. They took it in early so it could be put on the child's body before the service. As expected, the church pews were full to overflowing, and the hall overrun with flowers and candles. George sat in the front pew, alone. John and Barbara walked up and sat next to him.

The first service, for George's wife, put most of the audience in tears. The open casket holding her body sat on a raised platform on one side of the church, and that holding Elsie, on the other. The preacher stood at the podium between the two caskets. Aisles on both sides of the church and the large one between the pews were full to overflowing with well-wishers.

After the church services, the two caskets were carried outside and behind the church. Four parishioners lowered Mattie's casket into the ground in front of her headstone. George fell to his knees in tears. The marshal walked over to comfort him and help him up.

After prayers from the preacher, the congregation moved to the other side of the cemetery. There, two men closed the lid of a smaller casket with Ellie's body, dressed in her christening dress with a black bow. The service closed with words from the preacher. For the next hour well-wishers talked to George, the Marshal, and Barbara.

John and Barbara rode their buggy to Lake Tanganyika. They quietly sat in the carriage holding each other for the next half hour before returning to their farm. John pulled the buggy next to the barn while Barbara went inside to fix dinner. John unhitched the horse, and took him inside the barn where he fed and watered the animal. He then went into the house.

"That was a beautiful church service," John said. "I really felt sorry for George."

"I know, I felt the same," Barbara said. "I'm sure his feelings made it much worse knowing he had been responsible."

Several neighbors had brought in dishes and set them on the table on their way to the church services. John and Barbara both appreciated this greatly. After a fine meal, the two went in and enjoyed coffee in the living room. The Marshal held his wife, who leaned on his lap on the verge of tears.

"I don't understand why God did this to us," Barbara said. "I can't see where either of us deserved it."

"We didn't, and George certainly didn't," John said. "Nobody said life had to be fair. We have to move on."

After a short time, the two went into the bedroom, undressed, and slid under the covers together. They just held each other until sleep overtook them.

The next morning, John got up a little late and decided to let his wife sleep. It had been a hard night on both of them. He went out to the kitchen and brewed a pot of coffee, and after a couple of cups, left for the office. Frank had spent the night with the prisoners. Both outlaws would be taken to the train station, and transported to Kansas City, Missouri, for trial.

Al picked up the buckboard at the stable, and brought it to the office. He and Brett handcuffed the prisoners and escorted them outside. A few of the people on the stage-coach they had robbed were at the train station to give the two a fond farewell. One of the women went so far as to spit on Cantrell as he walked by.

After getting the two securely on the train, a couple of federal marshals from Kansas City took over their transport. Both men returned to the office. Al returned the buckboard to the stables. He felt relieved to get the outlaws out of his jurisdiction. Al came into the office. Brett and the Marshal were discussing the services held the day before.

"I wonder how George is going to get along," Al said. "It's bad enough losing somebody like that, but knowing you were responsible—I can't imagine what that must feel like."

"I know Barbara feels guilty over losing Ellie," the Marshal said. "But there's no way she was at fault. It was just a horrible accident."

"You plan on having another child?" Brett said.

"I talked to her about it, the Marshal said. "Like I told her, she needs a reason to go on. Neither of us will ever forget Ellie, but another child will provide company for her when I'm working."

Barbara came to the office a little later, bringing lunches for the Marshal and his deputies. She thanked each of them for the dishes their wives had left at the farm. She pulled roast pork sandwiches and potato salad out of the basket that she had brought. Al went over to the table on the other side of the room and poured coffee for the men.

"These sandwiches are sure good today," Fred said. "You need to give your recipe for the potato salad to my wife."

"Come on, Fred," Barbara said. "She could give me lessons when it comes to cooking. The sweet potatoes yesterday, were out of this world."

The Marshal spoke up. "Everything your wife's brought over yesterday tasted great, and was greatly appreciated. There's enough stuff there to last us the rest of the week."

After the men finished with their lunch, Barbara cleaned things up and went out to the buggy. John gave her a hug before lifting her onto the seat. There were no prisoners to watch or take care of, so the deputies went up the street to Jake's place for a beer. After finishing, the four deputies went out on their rounds. The Marshal and Al returned to the office. Things stayed quiet for the rest of the afternoon, with the exception of a couple of barroom brawls. Jake put a stop to those problems with "Old Betsy".

The stage from Austin, Texas pulled in a little later that afternoon. Eight passengers were taken off, and most headed for Jake's. Leonard took the coach back to the stable for a change of horses before picking up the passengers heading for Yuma. One of the men aboard the coach came over to the Marshal's office. John just finished posting his deputies timecards.

"Marshal, my name is Ellis Brewster. I'm a Marshal from the Oklahoma territory. I brought a few wanted posters, and thought I might leave them here. I'm heading for Phoenix this afternoon. I have an escaped prisoner with me, handcuffed inside of the coach. He's wanted for murder in Phoenix."

John looked at the four posters. "Any reason to think any of these guys may be coming this way?"

"Two of them have family in Tombstone. I doubt they'll be going there because from what I understand, they don't get along with their families."

"One of the men has a lady friend in that area, so it's possible he may want to see her. He's been in prison for the last five years, but managed to escape last month. He may want to look her up."

"After five years?" John said. "I would think she's probably moved on by now."

"I would think she probably has, but she was the one that turned him in. James has a hot temper and doesn't forget people that hurt him."

"Has she been told of his escape?" Al said.

"The authorities at the prison tried to send her a wire. We don't know whether or not it went through. We haven't gotten an answer."

"I think there may be a couple guys over at Jake's down from Tombstone. I'll check with them," Al said, and walked out.

Ellis Brewster stood up. "Well Marshal, I think I'll go grab a beer, and then head out."

John thumbed through the posters, and didn't see any familiar faces. He wanted his deputies to have a look at them, before showing them at Jake's, and posting them outside the Marshal's office.

Al came out of the saloon and back over to the office. John sat outside with his feet up on the hitching-rail.

"A couple of the guys knew the girl. Her name is Bessie Larson. They told me she got married and moved out of town. They didn't know where she went, but said they'd check around when they got back to Tombstone."

John tipped his hat as the stage left the depot. Several new passengers boarded the coach. John and Al watched as it disappeared down the street.

"Why don't you head for home, John?" Al said. "The boys and I can take care of anything that comes up until Les gets here."

"I think I'll do that. I don't like leaving Barbara alone any more than I have to right now."

The Marshal walked down to the stable and picked up his horse. He rode off heading for home. He got in a little earlier than usual, but figured that kind of made up for Saturday night. Barbara stood at the clothes-line out-doors taking down the weeks wash when John showed up.

He took the horse into the barn and fed him a bucket of oats. He gave the animal and their other horse a couple of apples, and walked out to the pump and got cleaned up. Barbara just finished pulling the wash off the clothes-line and carried the basket to the pump so John could take it in the house. He helped her fold the clothes and put them up. Afterward they went to the kitchen to decide what of several dishes given to them to fix.

"Aside from a couple of barroom brawls, things stayed pretty quiet in town," John said. "The stage came in. Paul and Ruth were on it. They just got back from her folks ranch. Ruth said to give you her regards. She was sorry to hear about Ellie."

"I wondered where they were. I haven't seen them in the last couple of weeks."

After a dinner of fried rice, rainbow trout, and all the fixings, John helped his wife clean up the kitchen before retiring to the living room sofa. The Marshal could tell his wife had almost come to terms with the loss of their daughter. They discussed the possibility of another child, and decided it would be a good idea. The two cleaned up and turned in early.

The next morning John got up and fixed a pot of coffee. He let Barbara sleep in, as she had taken laudanum the night before. He went out to the barn, saddled his horse, and rode to town. The stable hand told him about the robbery, and advised him to tie up at the hitching-post in front of the jail.

The marshal went in to find two men in the cells. He didn't recognize either of them. About that time he heard somebody come into the office.

"Good morning Marshal," Les said. "I just came over from Jake's. The bank was hit early this morning by four men. Two of them are back there in the jail cells."

"Are they talking?" John said.

"I haven't been able to get anything out of them," Les said. "Al got a couple of the boys and headed out after the other two."

John walked back to the cell holding the two men. He could see nervousness in them.

"My deputy said you don't want to say anything," the Marshal said. "I'll tell you something, you talk to me, and things will go a lot easier for you in court."

"We haven't got anything to say, Marshal," the larger man said. "We don't know where they're going."

"Al is one of my deputy Marshals. He's an Indian tracker, and you can believe me when I tell you, he'll find your friends."

John walked out to the outer office. "Les, why don't you go on home?" The Marshal said. "It's going to be a while before the other's get back. I can handle anything that happens before that."

"Brett should be here pretty soon. If you don't mind, I'll grab a beer at Jake's and head for home."

Les left the office as John went back to the cells. He handcuffed one of the men to the bars, and after handcuffing the other, pulled him out into the office.

"I don't know if your friend back there was speaking for you as well as himself," the Marshal said. "But, whoever talks first will have a lighter sentence than the other. I guarantee I'll get the truth out of one of you."

"I already told you Marshal, we don't know anything."

"You mean you don't know anything. Your friend back there looks kind of nervous. I haven't gotten the particulars on the robbery yet, so I don't know if you're looking at a rope or a long jail sentence."

John took the man outside and handcuffed him to the hitching rail, before going back to the cell to talk to his partner.

"I'm going to tell you the same thing I told your friend," John said. "I haven't got time for games. If anybody was killed in that robbery this morning, you'll both hang. If not, whoever talks first, will get a lighter sentence. We will get your friends."

The man looked at the Marshal. He could tell John meant business. He stayed quiet for a couple of minutes, and then spoke up.

"Trevor is the boss. He's one of the guys that got away."

"That's a good start, suppose you start by telling me who you are?"

"My name is Billy Ray Tomlin. The man, who escaped with Trevor, is my older brother, Richard. Silvio is the other man who's outside in your office. We didn't hurt anybody Marshal. We got there before the bank opened. Silvio blew the safe. We took a strong-box of gold and a duffel bag full of cash. That strong box is heavy, so I guess they must have unloaded the gold into their saddlebags. For some reason, Silvio's saddle must've been loose because he wound up on the ground. I went back to help him. Trevor and Richard took off down the road."

The Marshal got more information than he bargained for. He went out to the hitching-rail in front, and sat down next to his prisoner.

"Well, Silvio, your friend in there told me your saddle was loose, and you were dumped," John said. "Do you really think that was an accident?"

John could see the change in Silvio's expression. He sat there for a couple of minutes taking all of that in. The Marshal could see anger beginning to rage on the face of his prisoner.

"Trevor has a hideout this side of Tombstone. He's wanted for murder in Kansas, where he robbed a bank, and shot and killed the teller. From what I heard, he didn't have to do that."

The Marshal took his prisoner back inside the jail, this time putting him in a separate cell from his partner. Brett came in shortly after. John told him of the conversation with the prisoner.

"What do you think?" Brett said. "Should I get a couple of boys and head out to Tombstone?"

"If that's where they headed, I imagine Al probably has them in custody by now. If not, he'll track them to wherever they go."

Al and the two deputies tracked the men to their hideout just outside of Tombstone. They walked to the front door. The marshals heard the two men arguing. Al kicked in the front door. The outlaw shot Trevor in the heart as he drew on the deputies, killing him immediately. He threw his arms in the air when the deputy marshals aimed their guns at him. Al picked up the saddlebags with the gold and cash and strapped that onto the dead man's horse. Fred rode into Tombstone and told Pete to have the undertaker pick up Trevor's body.

The three deputy marshals took the outlaw, handcuffed to his saddle horn, and the horse with the gold and money and headed back to Tucson.

Later, Barbara showed up with enough lunch for six deputies. Shortly, the prisoners' lunch came over from the café. The man took the lunches into the jail, and returned shortly.

"Boy Marshal, those guys are sure pissed off at somebody."

"I imagine they are," John said. "I sure can't blame them."

After lunch, Barbara cleaned everything up, and John helped her out to the buggy. He watched as she disappeared down the street and then sat down on the bench in front of the jail, put his feet up, and enjoyed the sunny afternoon.

A couple hours later, Al and two deputies rode into town and to the stable. They left off the horses to be fed and watered, and took one of their prisoners to docs, and the other to the undertaker. Four saddlebags with gold and cash were strapped to the outlaw's horses.

"We recovered the gold and cash. The leader is dead. He pulled his gun on me, and his partner shot and killed him. I don't understand why he did that."

"I have a pretty good idea. Come on up to the jail, Barbara left lunches there for you," the Marshal said. "Brett, run the saddlebags up to the bank, and bring the horses back to the stable."

"Will do, John," Brett said. "I'm glad to see the rest of you made it back in one piece."

The Marshal spent the next half hour making out a full report on what happened that morning. A copy of the report would go by train to Kansas the next day with the prisoner.

Things stayed relatively quiet over the next couple of months. The summer season gave way to a colder autumn. The Marshal and his wife began to enjoy life a little more as time went on. John could see Barbara beginning to slow down.

"They're having a square dance in town tomorrow night," John said. "Do you think you might like to go?"

"That sounds lovely. We haven't done anything like that for a long time."

The next morning John let Barbara sleep in. He went to the kitchen, got coffee, and rode into town. The weather began getting colder at night and early in the morning. Al sat in the office when John came in.

"There was a shooting over at Jake's place this morning. A couple guys came in on the stage yesterday afternoon. I guess they were card cheats. One of the guys on the cattle drive called them on it. Details are pretty fuzzy after that. Two cattlemen are sitting in the jail."

John walked back to the jail and sat down outside the cell.

"Okay, what happened this morning?" The marshal said. "My deputies said something about gambling cheats."

"They were palming cards. Frank here saw one of them pulling cards out of his sleeve. A couple of the guys at the table got mad. One of the con-men stood up fast, lifting the table and dumping everything on the floor. He knocked two of us down and drew his gun and got off a shot."

"So you and Frank did what?" The Marshal said.

"Honest Marshal, if they hadn't drawn on us we wouldn't have shot back. One of the guys we shot is dead. The other one got the hell beat out of him. A couple of the guys carried him up to docs."

"You two cool your heels here while I go have a talk with Jake."

John walked out to the office. "Al, one of the other boys will be in here to relieve you. I need to go have a talk with Jake."

"No problem. I'm pretty sure Brett is across the street at Jake's."

The Marshal walked up the street and into the saloon. One of Jake's bartenders mopped up blood off the floor. Jake sat in front of the table, mending a leg that got broken in the scuffle. Brett talked to one of the other cattlemen. He turned when he saw the Marshal come in.

"John, from what I can tell those two we have locked up were just defending themselves. Don Conroy, one of the card sharks, is barely hanging on. The other one went to the undertaker."

The Marshal went across the street and released the two prisoners. He took their statements and they left. John walked down to the stables and went upstairs to the doctor's office.

"Morning Doc, I just came up to see how your patient is doing."

"I'm just waiting for a couple of stable hands to come up here and carry him to the undertaker. There wasn't much I could do."

"I guess it served them right. Barbara hasn't been feeling too well lately. I know part of it was probably Ellie, but she seems to be getting worse."

"She's not still on laudanum is she?" Doc said. "That's only for short-term use."

"No, she just used that stuff for about a week. I used it for a couple of nights. If she's not feeling better I may bring her by in the morning."

John went to the undertaker to get some information before returning to the office. He spent the next hour writing up the report.

Barbara came in a little later with lunch for her husband and his deputies. She said she felt a little better than she had that morning. After lunch she and John went to the general store to pick up some things, and then Barbara headed home. John sat down in front of the office at the hitching-post to soak up a little sun for an hour, and then went up the street for a beer, and to see Jake.

"Hello marshal," Jake said. "Here anything about Conroy?"

"Yeah, he's at the undertaker's. I guess there wasn't much Doc could do for him."

"Just as good, we sure don't need guys like that around. These men work hard for their money, and don't need somebody like that to steal it from them."

After a beer, John went back to the office. He always felt he did his job right when the jail cells were empty. The deputies returned from their rounds and enjoyed a cup of coffee.

Fred came in a little later to spell the guys for the night. John saddled up and went back to the farm. After putting his horse in the barn, he got cleaned up and went in the house and found Barbara back in the bedroom sleeping. He realized this wasn't like her at all. He quietly made his way to the kitchen where he fixed a pot of coffee. Shortly afterward Barbara came out and joined her husband.

"Honey, are you feeling okay?" John said.

"I've just been awfully tired the last couple of months, since Ellie died."

"I think it may be a good idea if I take you in to see the doc in the morning."

The two had a light meal that night. Barbara had been unable to eat most of hers. John helped her into the bedroom, and went back out to clean up the kitchen. When he finished, he went back into the bedroom and fell asleep next to his wife.

The next morning John got up and went out to the kitchen to fix coffee. He came back to the bedroom where Barbara sat on the edge of the bed. He helped her into the kitchen, where she got sick. John went out and hitched up a horse to the buggy. He put an overcoat around her helped her onto the buggy, and together they went into town. He pulled in at the stable and helped Barbara upstairs to the doctor's office while the stable attendants unhitched the horse.

"I don't know what's been happening, Doctor. I seem to be tired all the time, especially in the morning. I also get sick in the mornings."

The doctor had Barbara lie down on the table. He put his hands on her abdomen and began pushing slightly. He looked down at Barbara, and smiled.

"Mrs. Green, I do believe you are pregnant. I'm guessing about six weeks along."

Barbara looked up at John and beamed in delight. John bent over the table, and gave his wife a romantic kiss. The doctor gave her some medicine to take in order to ease the morning sickness.

"I guess I'll see you out at the farm about six months. In the meantime I want you to take it a little easier. You can still fix lunches for the marshals for a while until it gets to be too hard on you."

John went downstairs and had Cecil hitch up the horse to the buggy again.

The man looked at John. "Well I guess everything came out all right with the miss's at the doc's?"

"Everything's fine Cecil, it looks like we're pregnant again."

"Well I'm sure happy to hear that. I have a horse here you can use if you're going to stay here. I guess Barbara can handle the buggy okay?"

"I'll be fine, Cecil," Barbara said. "Say hi to Anna for me."

John helped his wife into the buggy. He watched as she rode down the street, stopping at the general store for supplies. She then left for the farm to get the lunches ready for the deputies that day.

John had Cecil saddle his horse, as he wanted to ride around town and check things out later that afternoon. He stopped by his office and went inside. Al and Brett were watching a prisoner that had tried to hold up the stage coming from Prescott that morning.

"I had to bring Barbara to the doc's office this morning. She's pregnant," John said. "What's this guy in here for?"

"I guess his gun jammed when he tried to hold up passengers on the stage this morning. He got on in Prescott. One of the passengers was able to get the gun away from him."

"So you tried to use the gun?" John said to the man.

"What difference does that make?"

"The difference is, the judge can throw an attempted murder charge at you, along with attempted robbery," John said. "The last time a stage was robbed, the gun didn't jam, and four men were hung."

The man sat back on the cot. The Marshal went out to the office putting the jail key in the desk drawer.

"That's good news about Barbara," Brett said. "Hopefully that will make her feel better."

The three law men got up and walked out to the porch and sat on the bench looking out over the town. Although being winter, the weather stayed warm during the day. Al and John walked across and up the street to Jake's for a beer. Brett stayed behind to watch the prisoner. They got back to the office shortly before Barbara showed up with lunch.

"You always seem to outdo yourself with these sandwiches. I'll have to tell the wife about this new relish you use," Deputy Martin said. "And as usual your tater salad is great."

"Thank you Josh, it's a new recipe," Barbara said. "Tell her to put a little horseradish in it."

After cleaning up the lunch basket, John helped Barbara out to the buggy and watched as she turned the buggy around and headed home. Leaving Brett in charge, the deputies left to their posts, and the marshal mounted his horse and made off for other parts of town. He liked to do this on occasion to keep in touch with friends and acquaintances around town, and check on any problems they may have. He rode up Congress Street stopping at the bank there. It had been held up the month before.

"How are you doing Hank," John said to the guard. "How's the arm?"

"It's doing a lot better now, John. I had a little hassle with a guy in here the other night. He wasn't armed, just a little drunk, so I told him to go home and sober up. I couldn't see much sense in arresting him."

"Did you know the guy?" John said.

"I've seen him around. Sometimes he hangs out in the saloon down the way."

"Well I'm glad you're feeling better, say hi to Marie for me." John said, tipping his hat, and walking out.

John mounted up and made a stop at the Sheriff's office and half a dozen more places before heading back to his office. The Sheriff's deputies around town were keeping everything pretty well in hand.

The marshall got back to the office late in the afternoon, and leaving Fred in charge, headed for home. Hearing a noise at the livery stable, John stopped to see if a problem needed to be taken care of. As he got off the horse, he heard a gunshot at the rear of the stables. He ran back there to find Cecil lying dead on bales of hay. He heard a noise in the back and ran out to see a man fleeing. He yelled at the guy, and then fired, hitting him in the shoulder and knocking him off the horse.

"Don't go for that gun, unless you don't want to wake up tomorrow," John said.

Probably thinking he would hang anyway, the man turned and fired at John, hitting him in the calf. John returned fire killing the man. Jerry, one of the bartenders at Jake's had just gotten off, and went to get his horse. Hearing the gunshots, he came running to the back of the stable. He passed the guy lying on the ground, and went over to the marshal. Jerry tied his bandanna around John's thigh, just below the knee, to stop the bleeding. He ran out and got a couple of men to take the Marshall to the doc's office, and then to the marshal's office to get Fred.

John had temporarily lost consciousness when he came into doc's office. Temporarily regaining consciousness, the marshall told Doc about Cecil. Doc went downstairs and got hold of the undertaker. They met in the stall where Cecil lay dead. The stable hand told the undertaker about the man in the back as well.

The undertaker went to the back, taking a couple of men with him to carry the body back to the cemetery, where they unceremoniously buried him. The undertaker then took Cecil's body to the funeral parlor.

Jerry told Al about the shooting. He went out to the farm to inform Barbara. She immediately got in the buggy and went to the doctor's office. She had Mac, at the stable, feed and water the horse.

She ran up the stairs and into his office "How is he, Amos?" Barbara said. "Can I see him?"

"He's unconscious right now. I gave him laudanum to relax him," the doctor said. "Why don't you wait out here until he comes to?"

"Do you have any idea how long that's going to be?"

"I would say at least a couple of hours."

"If that's the case, I'll go down to the café and get coffee," she said. "Can I get you anything?"

"No thanks, I have a pot of coffee up here. You're welcome to it."

"Thanks anyway, I just need to get out of here and clear my head for a while."

Barbara went downstairs to the cafe. Several people heard the news about her husband and came over to offer their condolences. She cried softly between these encounters. She then got up and started walking around town trying to keep her mind off what had happened. Several of the deputies stopped her to get any information they could about John. Walking back she met Brett.

"Do you have news on my husband?" She said, almost dreading an answer.

"I just came from there. He's weak and in pain, but awake. He asked about you."

In most cases she would consider that good news, but she realized in this case it probably wouldn't be, as she seldom knew about any injuries to her husband until he got home. She hurriedly made her way up the stairs to the doctor's office.

"John's awake and asking for you," the doctor said. "You can go in, but be careful not to excite him. He's lost a lot of blood."

"Will he be okay?" Barbara said.

"He well, but it'll take time. I was able to save the leg, but he's going to need to work it."

Barbara went into the room where her husband lay on the bed in pain.

"John, the doctor says you're going to be fine," Barbara said. "It's going to take a little time for your leg to heal."

"Yeah, about two months, he wants me to stay off of it altogether for about three weeks," John said. "Do you think you can put up with me that long?"

"I don't know, but we can give it a try. The doc said you'd have to spend the night here. I'll bring the buggy out in the morning and pick you up."

Barbara went to the general store to pick up laudanum, bandages, tape, and a few other things she'd need to take care of John's needs for the next couple of weeks. She took the buggy back to the farm. After putting the horse up, she went in the house. Not being in much of a mood to eat, she went in and lay on the bed. It had been a hard day for her, and tears came to her eyes as she thought about the pain her husband must be feeling.

The next morning Barbara got up and, after breakfast, went out to the barn and hitched the horse to the buggy. A light wind started blowing kicking up a lot of sand, making the trip to town a little uncomfortable. Getting into town, she had a stable hand give the horse a bucket of oats. She went up the stairs to the doctor's office.

"How's my husband doing Amos?"

"His fever pitched overnight. I had to go in and do more work on his leg. He's going to have to stay here at least until tomorrow."

As he expected, Doc realized this news caused Barbara a lot of anguish. He sat her down and tried to calm her before she left. John's condition would have to improve before she could see him. She left the office and went back to the stable. She returned to the farm, fixing lunch for the deputies, and returned to town about noon.

"I saw John at doc's office a few minutes ago," Al said. "He's pretty well out of it right now. Doc told him you were there early this morning, but I don't know if he understood."

"That laudanum is pretty strong stuff. I can't take him home until at least tomorrow. I guess Doc told you he'd be off work for a couple of months."

"Yeah, I'll believe that when I see it," Brett said, as he came in the office. "I know your husband better than that."

"Well, Doc made it pretty clear that he better take it easy unless he wants to walk with a limp for the rest of his life."

Jerry followed a couple more deputies into the jail, bringing lunches to two prisoners. After the lunch break, Brett stayed with the office while Al and the others left to patrol the town.

Barbara stopped at the doc's office to see the marshal. Although conscious, he barely recognized his wife. Barbara talked to the doctor for a few minutes to be sure she understood how to take care of her husband once she got him back home. She got the buggy downstairs, and went back to the farm.

Brett took over John's duties as U.S. Marshal until he returned to the office. Aside from a few bar fights, most of which were handled by his deputies, things stayed pretty quiet in Tucson over the next few days.   Barbara had taken John back to the farm for his recuperation. They both realized he would have to stay quiet and in bed for at least the rest of the week.

Barbara came into his bedroom. "I'll have breakfast here in a few minutes." She said. "Are you feeling better this morning?"

"Much better, that medicine doc gave me helps the pain a lot, but it wears off too soon. I think I'm going to cut down on it."

"Well, you know how you feel. As Amos told you, you need to take it easy and let me help you any way I can. I talked to Brett while I was in town yesterday. He told me to tell you not to worry, things are running smoothly."

Following the doctor's orders, John reluctantly stayed in bed for the next five days.

In the meantime, a gang of four men held up one of Tucson's banks. It contained the payroll for several of the large ranches. Brett and two of his deputies got descriptions from the bank and rode after the outlaws heading for Yuma and catching up with them when they stopped for the night at a roadhouse. One of the deputies went to the rear of the single-story building. Brett and Al slowly made their way to the front door.

Looking through a front window Brett could see the four men sitting at a table, drinking and gambling. He recognized one of the men from the description given to him at the bank. Several other patrons sat at the bar. The two law men went in, keeping their badges out of sight.

They went over to a table next to the outlaws. Fred came into the room through the back door, and made his way to the table where Brett and Al sat. The three slowly drew their guns and put them on the outlaws.

"Quietly put your guns on the floor and don't try anything cute," Al said. "You're all under arrest for bank robbery."

Realizing they had no choice, the outlaws followed Al's orders. One at a time the four men stood up and were handcuffed.

Fred kept an eye on the other patrons, while Brett and Al led the four men to the room they had rented for the night. After securing the four, the law men brought in their bed rolls, as it had gotten late and dark. The outlaws, handcuffed to the beds, slept on the floor.

Early the next morning, after a decent breakfast of eggs, oatmeal and coffee, the four men were put on their horses and taken back to Tucson. The law men carried the saddlebags full of money.

The six got back to Tucson about noon and the four outlaws were jailed. The deputies returned the money to the bank. There were no injuries, aside from a clerk one of the outlaws had hit with his gun.

"Al, why don't you and Fred get yourselves a beer while I fill out the paperwork?" Brett said.

"Sounds like a plan. Can we bring you anything?"

"No thanks, Barbara should be getting here soon with our lunches."

The two deputies returned to the jail shortly before Barbara got there. Lunches for the four outlaws were brought in from across the street and taken back to them.

"How's John getting along?" Brett said. "We miss him around here, but don't tell him I said that."

"He's out of bed now and as you can imagine, getting antsy, and wants to get back to work."

"Frankly, knowing John, I'm surprised he's not already here."

"The doctor told him what would happen if he tried anything like that. I'll see to it he does what he's told."

"Well, I wish you luck," Al said. "I've known John a long time and as you know he can be kind of stubborn sometimes."

Barbara shook her head affirmatively. She then took the plates and silver back to the buggy, and headed back to the farm after stopping at the general store for a few supplies.

The next morning, Brett handcuffed the four prisoners. Fred brought up the buckboard and loaded the prisoners onto it. Al stayed behind to watch the jail. The outlaws were taken to the courthouse where they stood trial for bank robbery. They were all sentenced to ten years hard labor at the Yuma federal penitentiary.

Chapter 7

Back at the farm, John began to get around a little easier, having sworn off taking any drugs unless necessary. Being able to walk with the help of a crutch, his recovery seemed to be going a little better than the doctor predicted.

"You know, honey," John said. "If I keep this up I should be able to get back to work sooner than Doc said."

"He also told you not to rush it. You don't want to be crippled up for life."

John looked lovingly at his wife. She went to the kitchen and began preparing lunches for the deputies. She enjoyed doing this as it gave her a feeling of being needed. Besides, she enjoyed getting out and seeing some of her friends in town on occasion.

Barbara hitched up the buggy and drove into town. She parked in front of the Marshall's office and took the basket into the men waiting for her.

"Hello Barbara," Al said. "How's John getting along?"

"You know John. He's antsy to get back to work. He seems to be getting along better, and walking a little easier."

Lunch came in from across the street and Dennis took it into the jail for a couple of men that had gotten into bar fights at Jake's place the night before. Dennis returned to the office a few minutes later.

"I guess Pete and Roy got into it again last night," Dennis said. "They're good friends until they get liquored up. How's John getting along?"

"Like I was just telling the deputies," Barbara said. "He's anxious to get back to work. He'll be off a while longer."

Dennis smiled, "well tell him I said hi."

After feeding the four deputies, Barbara cleaned up and went back to her buggy. After a stop at the general store, she headed back to the farm. She put the buggy away and took the supplies into the house. John called her into the living room.

"How's everything in town?" John said. "I've been exercising my leg as much as I can."

"Pete Burton and Roy Weaver got in a fight again last night. Brett says he's going to keep them overnight this time."

"That's probably a good idea. Those two I don't understand, when they're sober they're the best of friends. Their fights seem to get worse, one of these days only one of them is going to walk away."

"Brett said he told them that last night," Barbara said. "I know you've told them that before."

"More times than I care to count, are the rest of the guys okay?"

"Al's shoulder got a little banged up last night when he went to bring them in. That's the main reason Brett decided to keep them another day. They agreed to pay Jake for the damages to the chairs. Pete tried to crack Roy over the head, but hit the bar instead."

John and Barbara settled into a nice dinner of roast goose. Afterwards John made his way back to the living room, while Barbara cleaned up in the kitchen. She came into the living room to join her husband for a bottle of wine. They spent a good part of the rest of the night thinking of a name for their new baby when it comes.

Fred relieved Al in the Marshall's office. Things stayed quiet until early the next morning. Jenny Rawlings came running into the office.

It took her a minute to catch her breath. "Fred, there's been a holdup at the assay office. Nobody was in there, so nobody was hurt," Jenny said. "According to Jake Sanders, three men blew up the safe."

"Did he happen to say which way they headed?"

"Said they took off out of town going west, but from there, he didn't know."

Fred got a part-time deputy over at Jake's to watch the office, then went down to the stable and got his horse. He began riding west, stopping at Al's ranch and picking him up. The two rode off following the tracks of the horses. They headed north toward Phoenix. Al could tell their directions by the depth of the horse's hooves. The marshal's caught the three in a Phoenix saloon. Their horses were still saddled in front. Hiding their badges, Al and Fred made their way to the bar. One man stood at the bar with a beer.

Fred walked over to the bartender and quietly asked what three men had come in together. Overhearing them, the man at the bar started to pull his gun on Al. Fred cracked him over the head with his gun from behind. He immediately turned around and turned his gun on two men at the table. Al went over and handcuffed the two, taking their guns. Fred handcuffed the man on the floor as well and the two were taken out and tied to their saddles, the man from the floor, thrown over his horse.

The two law men handcuffed the three to their beds in a Phoenix hotel and spent the rest of the night. They left early the next morning.

The five got back to Tucson the following day as Barbara brought in lunches for the men. Fred went across the street and ordered lunches for the three prisoners. None had taken time for breakfast that morning.

Barbara noticed the dust all over Fred and asked what happened. He spoke up.

"The assay office was held up day before yesterday by those three. We chased them clear to Phoenix, we just got back. We spent last night on the trail."

"That's over a 100 miles from here. You must've raced to get here in time for lunch," Barbara said. "I hope it's worth it."

Fred spoke up. "It always is. Al took the gold back to the assay office. He should be getting here pretty quick."

Barbara just got the spread out on the table when Al came in, covered in trail dust as well. After getting coffee for everybody, he sat at the table. A couple minutes later Dennis came in with lunches for the three men in the jail cells.

"John's been working hard to get back here," Barbara said. "I do wish he'd take it a little easier, but you guys know how he is."

"Only too well," Al said. "I'm surprised he's stayed quiet as long as he has. You might tell him we have everything covered here and not to worry."

"When is the circuit judge due here?" Dennis said, coming from the jail cells. Those guys look a little mean."

"Well, Dennis, I guess I'd be mad too. We kind of screwed up their plans for a happy life. I guess the state will keep them fed and clothed for the next few years."

"That's one way of looking at it," Dennis said as he left the office. "I'm not sure they'll agree with you."

After lunch, Al helped Barbara back to the buggy. She left heading back to the farm. Al walked back into the office. He and Fred both headed home as Brett entered the room. Taking the notes from the desk Al had left, Brett began filling out the papers for court the next morning.

Hearing the gunshots over at Jake's, Brett strapped on his gun and ran across the street to the saloon. A man bleeding badly from his chest fell from the batwing doors out onto the boardwalk. He didn't recognize the man and slowly made his way to the doors. He could hear yelling inside and looked over the doors. A man with a gun stood next to a table.

"You all saw it, he drew on me and I was protecting myself," the man yelled. "I'm going to walk out of here now, don't nobody try to follow me."

Brett backed away from the door and waited for the man to come out and when he did the marshal coldcocked him with his pistol, knocking him to the ground. He called into the saloon to let the people know he had the man in custody. He picked the man up after handcuffing him and led him across the street to the jail. He hadn't counted on the guy's partner, who came out and shot the marshal in the back.

"Everybody stay in the saloon and nobody will get hurt," the man said as he walked over and took the handcuffs off his friend.

He helped his friend on the horse and the two rode out of town together. Brett lay bleeding on the street. Jake and a couple of his customers ran over to Brett while another went to get the doc. Alex came down from his office and ran over to Brett.

"He's got a very weak pulse," the doctor said. "A couple of you get him up to my office. You better call the undertaker for the other man."

Two of the cowboys lifted Brett from the dirt Street and carried him down the road and up the stairs to the doctor's office. The doc followed them, having them lay him down on the bed in the examining room. They left and went back to the saloon. Jake and two deputies went through the door of the doctor's office, and into the examining room.

"Can you tell anything yet, Doc?" Jake said. "Is he going to be okay?"

"It doesn't look good. He's lost a lot of blood," the doc said. "I won't know much till morning. In the meantime, you better try to get hold of Al."

Jake went back to the saloon and sent one of the men to find Al and Fred and bring them to the saloon. Al picked up Fred on the way and they rode at full gallop to the saloon.

"Anybody see which way the two went?" Al said. "I'm going to need a couple of you men to join us."

A couple of the Marshall's part-time deputies were in the bar. They were able to tell Al which way the men rode off. The four deputies rode off going east, taking out after them. A sandstorm that morning made tracking them much easier. They got to the turnoff going up to Tombstone and saw that the two outlaws had continued going east.

The Marshal's continued following them until early evening. They had stopped to rest and water their horses and sat at a campfire with coffee. Hearing the beats of the horses, the two pulled rifles from their saddles and shot and killed **Fred** and one of the deputies. Al and the other deputies pulled off the road behind heavy brush.

Taking careful aim, Al shot and killed one of the men. The other ran for his horse. Al took careful aim at the man as he ran and yelled for him to stop. He started to mount his horse and Al fired at him, hitting him in the shoulder.

The other deputy ran up to the man with his gun drawn and warned him not to try anything. They took the man into custody and tied him to his horse they threw the other man over the saddle of his horse. Both Fred and the other marshal, whom the outlaws had killed, were also thrown over the saddles of their horses.

Although tired from the nights ride, the two marshals took the four back to Tucson. They got in late in the afternoon and took the three men to the undertakers. The two deputies took the outlaw to the jail. Les had come in the night before and watched the office. Al and the other deputy headed home. Al had the unpleasant task of talking to Fred's wife as well as the wife of the other deputy.

John had found out about the shootings in the saloon the day before when his wife had gone into town. Carlos rode out to their farm to let John know what had happened.

"I'm sorry to be the one to tell you this John," Carlos said. "Fred and Steve Milner were both killed going after the two men from the saloon the other day."

"Oh, God! Have their wife's been notified?" John said.

"Yeah, Al said he'd take care of it," Carlos said. "That's one job I'd never want to do."

After Carlos left for town, John went back to the bedroom to see Barbara. She lay on the bed, tired from taking the lunches to the jail, cleaning up, and coming back.

"Carlos was just here," John said. "Steve Milner and Fred were both killed going after the two that shot Brett."

"Oh no," Barbara said, tearing up. "Has anybody let their wife's know?"

"Yeah, Al's taking care of it. I just feel so helpless."

"I know, John, but the men were just doing their job. Your being in the office wouldn't have changed that."

John patted her on the shoulder and limped out of the room. He went to the living room and sat on the sofa. His mind flooded with thoughts about what it must've been like for Fred and the deputy out on the trail. Now there were two more funeral services to attend.

"Have you heard how Brett's getting along?" John said.

"I talked to his wife this morning," Barbara said. "The doctor said she could take him home tomorrow morning if he was up to it."

"That's a relief," John said. "From what Carlos said, I guess it was touch and go for a while."

The Circuit Judge came into town the next morning. Al and Les took the prisoner by buckboard to the courthouse leaving Frank in charge of the office. The two marshals went into the courtroom to give testimony. The judge walked into the court minutes later after the outlaw had been cleaned up and brought in.

"You're charged with murder of a man in Jake's bar and with the attempted murder of a Deputy Marshal. How do you plea?"

"I didn't kill the man, my partner did. He also shot the Deputy Marshal."

"You realize when a murder is committed, everybody involved is considered guilty whether or not you actually pull the trigger. I hereby sentence you to hang by the neck until you are dead."

Les and Al handcuffed the prisoner and took him back to the jail. The next morning a good number of the townspeople were there to see the hanging. The outlaw was taken up the steps to the gallows and a noose put over his head. After last rites, the hangman pulled the lever and the floor fell out from under the condemned man.

The undertaker had a couple men load the corpse onto his buckboard and take him to the cemetery for an unceremonious burial.

John's health continued to improve over the next couple of weeks. He began to make the trips to town with Barbara with lunch for the deputies.

Things had been reasonably quiet aside from a few brawls in the bar. The cattle drive out of Kansas City resulted in a few arrests for drunk and disorderly and two for shooting up Jake's saloon. That had been taken care of when Al put the two in jail and, the trail boss agreed to pay damages to Jake. After that a deputy had been assigned to stay in the bar, at the expense of the trail boss, while the cattlemen were in town.

John noticed that Barbara began to slow down and started to show. They were both anxious for the birth of their new child. John's health improved to the point where he could go into the office, providing he stay off the leg as much as possible. He took care of all the office work including taking care of the paperwork of the criminal cases that came across his desk. Things had been reasonably quiet once the cattle drive continued on to the West Coast. There were enough barroom brawls around the town to keep the marshals busy.

John heard gunfire coming towards him down the street and made his way out to the boardwalk in time to see three men riding at full gallop coming toward him. Minutes later Al and Les were following them. Les continued on and Al stopped when he saw John outside.

"*Those three just held up the bank on Congress St.,*" Al said. "*They* shot and killed the bank guard."

The marshal watched as Al rode off down the street. He walked over to Jake's and asked a couple off-duty deputies to follow the deputy marshals in case they needed help. The men were happy to comply and were soon on their way.

"What's going on, John?" Jake asked. "I heard something about a bank robbery this morning. Jack, sitting at the table over there is pretty badly shaken up. He was at the bank at the time."

John walked over to the table, "Jack, Jake tells me you witnessed the bank robbery this morning. Did you recognize any of them?"

"I didn't really see much, Marshal. One of the men shot Chester on their way out. I'm not sure, but I think he recognized one of them."

"How's that?" The Marshal said.

"Just a feeling, when Chester looked up at the guy, they seemed to recognize each other. That's when the outlaw shot him and ran out."

The Marshal returned to the office. His leg still bothered him to the point where he couldn't ride comfortably. He walked back to the jail cells and saw a man asleep on the bunk in the end cell.

"Okay Jess, on your feet. You got enough hospitality out of us. Go on home the next time you feel like getting drunk, do it there."

Jesse got up and walked out of the cell. "I didn't mean to get drunk Marshal. Betty kept passing me drinks."

"Yeah, well next time take it a little easier. You owe Jake for a new barstool and a couple of glasses. Take it up with him."

Jesse walked out the door of the jail and up the street to square things with Jake. John went over to his desk and began filling out paperwork that he would need when Al and Les would bring the three outlaws into town later. After finishing the office work John went outside to the bench and decided to enjoy the warm weather.

"Good morning, Marshal," Millie Hicks said. "How's your leg doing?"

"Morning Millie—Abigail," John said. "It's doing much better, thanks. It's still a little sore to try to ride a horse. Doc says in a couple of weeks he'll take the cast off."

"Well, you take it easy and say hello to Barbara for us," Millie said, continuing on down the sidewalk heading to the general store.

About that time John saw his wife coming down the street in the buggy. She had brought lunches down for the men. She pulled up in front of the marshal's office and John went over to help her down.

"Les and Al are out chasing down three men that robbed the bank this morning. Frank and Ed went out to help them as well. I don't know what time they'll be back."

"Well, if you can take this basket inside, I think I'll go see the doctor while we wait for them to get back."

John took the basket inside and then walked out helped his wife off the buggy and up to the doc's office. The doctor again warned him about using the leg any more than necessary. Not wanting to leave the office empty, the marshal went back.

About an hour later John saw his deputies coming back. Two of the outlaws lay dead over their saddles. Les had his arm in a makeshift sling. They stopped in front of the undertaker's office and left off the two dead men and then Les stopped at the doctor's office. Al brought his prisoner to the jail.

"I see Les got hurt," John said. "What happened out there?"

"We caught up with them just past the road to Tombstone," Al said. "When they saw us they turned around and fired. Les and I returned fire. One of them dropped to the ground, the other two kept going. We followed him, he turned around, fired and I brought him down with the rifle. The other turned around and gave himself up."

"Was les hurt very badly?" John said.

"I don't think so. I put my bandanna around his arm and propped it up. He should be back pretty quick."

The marshal saw his wife coming out of the general store up the street. She walked down the boardwalk to John's office. She went in and set things up for the lunches. The two deputy marshals John had called on to backup Al and Les returned to the office. Not being trackers, they had taken the road up to Tombstone and returned once they realized their mistake. They saw the dust from the horses heading back to Tucson, and saw Al and Les with their quarry. Al walked to the café across the street and ordered lunch for the outlaw.

Barbara started putting lunch out for the men when Les walked in. His arm in a sling didn't seem to bother him. He sat down with the other marshals.

"How's the arm doing?" John said.

"It doesn't feel too bad right now. Doc said it was just a flesh wound. He pulled the bullet out and put my arm in a sling. He said it'd be all right in a day or two."

"These roast beef sandwiches are sure good," Al said. "And so is that tater salad."

A few minutes later Frankie brought in lunch for the prisoner. He came back into the office shortly.

"That tough prisoner of yours back there is crying," Frankie said. "Guess I can't blame him."

"He hasn't got much of a future," Les said. "One of those three killing the bank guard saw to that."

"I guess he'll try to put it on one of the others," the marshal said. "There was a witness, but it won't make much difference who did the shooting."

After lunch John helped Barbara get things cleaned up and helped her out and onto the buggy. He watched his wife as she turned the buggy around and headed back to the farm.

The Marshal sent Les home for the day. Al and one of the off-duty deputies taking Les' place began doing their rounds. The Marshal walked back to the cell holding the prisoner. He was lying on his side facing the brick wall. He turned over when he heard John come in.

"Which one of you killed Chester?" John said. "He had a wife and two kids you know. Don't try to lie to me. We have a witness that can identify the murderer."

"It was Alias, he and Chester were cousins."

John shook his head and walked back out to his desk. The circuit court would be in session the next day. Rather than pulling his witness into court, John figured it would be easier to have him identify one of the three before the court proceedings. The marshal realized that it wouldn't make much difference anyway. He sent for Jack at his home.

Jack came in a little later and walked to the end cell with John.

"No, he wasn't the one that killed Chester."

Al walked Jack down to the undertaker's office. They went into the back room where two bodies lay covered on the table. Elias pulled back the cover.

"That's the one that did it," Jack said, pointing at one of the outlaws. "How could somebody do something like that to their kin?"

"They call it self-preservation," Al said. Thanks Doc, you can bury them now. You'll probably have another customer day after tomorrow."

Al and Jack walked over to Jake's for a beer. After a quick one, Al went to the office and told the marshal the murderer had been identified. He then returned to his duties.

John wrote up the paperwork including an affidavit that Jack had signed at the corners office. The trial would be held the next morning. The outlaw in the marshal's cell had that lifeless look in his eyes that told John he could've just as easily killed the guy.

Later that afternoon Frank came in to relieve John for the night. Al had not returned. Barbara had brought the buggy up to pick John up to take him back to the farm. John went to the pump and took off his shirt to get cleaned up while Barbara put the buggy up.

The two walked into the house. Two men were inside waiting for them. One of the men threw Barbara to the floor. The other grabbed John behind the neck.

"We don't want no trouble mister. Just tell that pretty wife of yours to fix us up some grub. You give me any trouble and I'll break the other leg."

Barbara looked up at the man. "Who are you and what do you want?"

"Never you mind, Missy. You two just do what we tell you, and you won't get hurt. Like I said, fix us some grub!"

The men came over to where his partner still held John and tied his hands behind his back. They took them over and threw him on a kitchen chair and tied him to it. Barbara then went into the kitchen to prepare a meal. While the two men ate, Barbara went over to help feed her husband. John shook his head no and mouthed. Don't say anything.

"My husband's leg needs attention and his hands are getting numb. Please let me help him."

One of the men looked at her. "Okay, but don't try anything."

Barbara untied her husband and freed his hands and legs. The two men were too busy eating to notice her as she untied his bonds.

One of the men came over to Barbara. "What say we go in the other room and have a little fun? Jacob, come over here and watch this guy. I'll be back in a few minutes.

John looked at the man. "You leave her alone, she's pregnant, can't you see that?"

The man slapped John on the face. "I'll do what I damned well please. Jacob get over here!"

Jacob came over and John waited until the man left the room with Barbara. Jacob got a little close, and John's fist immediately put him on the floor. He got up, pulled a pistol out of the drawer, and went into the bedroom where the man had thrown his wife on the bed. He saw John come in the door with a gun in his hand and froze.

John yelled, "Marshal John Green, put your hands over your head—and I mean now."

The man rolled over and off the bed making the mistake of pulling his gun. John shot and killed the man before he could do anything. Barbara ran up to her husband and threw her arms around him, sobbing. The two walked out to the living room where the other man had just come to.

"Put your hands in the air and don't try anything. Your partner's dead because he did."

The man slowly threw his gun across the room and then got up off the floor. "Don't shoot mister, we just wanted grub."

"Yeah, if that's all your partner wanted, you both might've walked out of here."

John threw the man on the chair and tied him to it securely. Barbara then had dinner on before the two retired to the bedroom. John pulled the man out into the living room in front of his partner throwing a rug underneath him to keep the floor clean.

The next morning Barbara went out to the kitchen to fix coffee. The man in the chair looked half alive. She could've cared less. John came out, had coffee and light breakfast before tying his prisoner to the saddle horn on his horse, and the other over the saddle on the one he had ridden.

He kissed his wife goodbye and proceeded to lead the other two horses into town. He stopped at the undertaker's, where he dropped off the dead body, and took the other prisoner to the jail.

"Getting started a little early aren't you John?" Frank said. "Where'd you get this guy?"

"He and his partner were in my home when we got there last night. They tied me to a chair, and the dead one tried to have his way with Barbara."

Frank laughed. "I take it they didn't know who you were?"

"No, I guess not. I may need you to stick around a while. Frank and I have to take a prisoner to court this morning. I guess I'll take our new guest with us as well."

The Marshal took his prisoner into the jail while Frank went to the stable for the wagon. Al stayed with the jail in case somebody needed him. John didn't bother to take the handcuffs off his prisoner. He ordered the other man over to the cell bars, where he put the handcuffs on the man. When

Frank came in, he unlocked the cell and John took the prisoner's out to the wagon. Frank tied his horse behind the wagon.

The marshals took the men down to the courthouse and then inside to be cleaned up and processed. Frank returned to his duties and John went into the courtroom. Shortly afterward both prisoners were brought into the court to stand trial. The circuit Judge entered the courtroom shortly afterward.

The man who had broken into John's home and tried to hold him and his wife hostage, went first. The judge spoke up.

"Young man, you're charged with the kidnapping of a Federal marshal and assault on him and his wife," the Judge said. "Enter your plea."

"Honest judge, we didn't know the man was a federal marshal. We just wanted something to eat and a place to stay for the night. Tommy was the one that tried to hurt the marshal's wife. I didn't have anything to do with it."

"According to the marshal you did nothing to try to stop it. If the marshal's wife hadn't been able to free her husband before she was taken into the bedroom, I suspect the law would have been hunting you both for murder."

"Oh no judge, you've got it wrong. All we wanted was something to eat and a place to stay."

"I guess you just picked the wrong place to stop," the Judge said, smiling. "The marshall told us what happened in the affidavit. Had you had anything to do with the assault on his wife, you can believe me when I tell you, your sentence would've been much harsher. I sentence you to 10 years at the Yuma federal prison— next case."

Marshals accompanied the convicted man out of the courtroom, and brought the man in on the bank robbery charge.

"You've been charged with bank robbery and the murder of the bank guard," the judge said. "What's your plea?"

The man looked at the judge and then at John. "I was in on the bank robbery Your Honor, but I had nothing to do with the murder. One of the other guys killed the man, because the guard recognized him. In fact it was his cousin."

"Well Mister Reese, as you may or may not know, who killed the guard has little to do with your sentence," the judge said. "You are hereby sentenced to be taken to the gallows tomorrow morning and be hung by the neck until you are dead. May God have mercy on your soul."

The marshals took the man from the courtroom, placed him in cuffs, and took him out to the wagon along with the other prisoner. Frank stopped by a few minutes later and helped the other deputy marshal to load the prisoners. He got up on the seat with John, and stopped at the train depot to unload the man sentenced to Yuma territorial prison. Frank stayed with the prisoner until the train would pick him up.

John returned to the office where Al put the convict in jail and picked up the wagon, returning it to the stable. He came back shortly, and went back to see the prisoner. The man refused to say anything and Al went back out into the office.

"What happened to the other prisoner?" Al said.

John looked up, "he was sentenced to 10 years hard labor. After what he and his partner did, it's hard for me to feel sorry for him."

"I can't say as I blame you, Al said. "I think if they'd come into my home and done anything like that, they'd probably both be dead."

John began getting the paperwork ready for the next day. Al went out on rounds. He and the other deputies came back to the office about noon. Frank came in shortly after Barbara got there.

"I guess you took care of getting our prisoner off on the train?" John said. "Did he give you any trouble?"

"Handcuffed the way he was, hardly," Frank said. "He thought the judge went a little hard on him. I told him he was lucky you didn't shoot him instead of bringing him in for trial."

John looked at him. "Truthfully, that was a close call. If Barbara had been hurt in any way, he never would've seen the inside of the courtroom."

Barbara looked up at him. "Yeah, sure, come on John, I think we all know you better than that."

After a lunch of deviled eggs and ham sandwiches, the deputies went back to work. John pulled his wife to him and gave her a long kiss. He then escorted her out to the buggy and watched as she turned it around and headed back to the farm.

Things stayed quiet in Tucson that afternoon. Jerry got there a little early for the night shift. The marshal decided to leave early, as he worried about his wife. Dust storms had been coming and going most of the day. Luckily, the weather had cleared up before John left. He went to the stable, were Josh had fed and saddled the marshal's horse.

After putting the horse away and getting cleaned up the marshal went into the house. Barbara had a dinner of fried chicken and dumplings waiting for John when he got home that evening.

"You always seem to outdo yourself," John said. "That dinner was delicious. Thank you. Why don't you go back and lay down, I'll clean things up."

"Thank you, honey. I think I'll take you up on that."

After cleaning up the kitchen John went into the bedroom and lay next to his wife. They talked for a while before Barbara fell asleep. John quietly got up and went into the other room. After a couple of beers, he went back into the bedroom. Barbara had gotten up, changed and went to bed. John did the same.

The next morning John quietly got up, letting Barbara sleep. He left a note for her saying he'd get lunches for the deputies across the street and not to worry about it. After a cup of coffee, he left for town.

After a cold, dusty ride John arrived at the stable where he put up the horse, walked to the office and relieved Jerry. When the weather warmed up, Al and John handcuffed the prisoner and took him from his cell to the courtyard behind the jail. Several family members and friends of the bank guard he had killed waited patiently for the prisoner to be brought out.

John walked Reese up the 13 steps of the gallows. The marshal turned the prisoner over to the hangman. The minister said a few kind words and turned Reese over to be hung. The hangman carefully placed the prisoner over a trapdoor, asking if there were any last words. When the man refused the hangman slipped the noose over the condemned man's neck and a hood over his head. He pulled the lever, dropping Reese to his death. A loud roar of applause and yelling came from the crowd as John and Al returned to the office.

Things stayed pretty quiet around Tucson for the next couple of days. John could tell Barbara had gotten close to her due date, and figured he'd better start thinking about taking time off to be with her for the birth of their new child. He waited until Brett returned to work.

Three days later Brett came back to work. The doctor told him he would have to take it easy for short time, but he assured John he could handle anything that came in. The marshal realized he would be more than able to do that and decided to take time off until the baby came.

John went to the stable, picked up his horse and went back to the farm. The weather was beginning to turn cold as he got back to the farm. He put up his horse, cleaned up at the pump and went into the house. He found Barbara in the back room lying down. John lay down with her for a few minutes, got up and went into the kitchen. He fixed a meal for the two of them and took it into the bedroom. He noticed her cramping more and more often. After a quiet meal of ham hock and lima beans, he took the dishes back to the kitchen, cleaned things up and returned to the bedroom.

"I can feel the baby kicking now and I think you're coming close to being a father. Thelma has been checking in on me a couple times a day. She helped deliver Junes child and said she would help with ours as well."

John looked down at his wife and could see her in pain. "I think it may be a good idea if I go get her now. She can stay here overnight just in case you need her."

John went outside and hooked up the buggy and took it over to Brett's farm where he picked up Thelma and returned to find Barbara in pain. Thelma went into the bedroom and talked to her, while John put the buggy up. Thelma came out to the living room and sat down on the sofa.

"She's not quite ready to deliver, but I'm glad you went over and picked me up," Thelma said. "I think you can plan on being a father sometime tomorrow."

"We really appreciate this, Thelma," John said. "I had a feeling by the way Barbara talked that she was getting close."

John set up the second bedroom for Thelma to use that night. He threw a couple blankets on the couch where he would stay. He had a restless night.

The next morning Brett went into the office to relieve the deputy. Al showed up shortly afterward. There were a couple guys sleeping off their activities at the bar the night before. They hadn't done any damage so Brett sent them home with a warning.

Al got one of the other deputies to watch the jail for a short time. He and Brett walked over to Jake's saloon up the street. They both got a beer and sat at the bar.

Brett looked at his partner. "Al, I can tell something's been bothering you this morning, what's going on?"

"I don't understand that wife of mine," Al said. "First she tells me she wants another kid, then she tells me she can't keep up with the ones we have."

"Look Al, if we're going to try to unravel female logic, we're going to need stronger drinks."

"Brother, you can say that again!" Al said.

About that time the marshals heard gunfire from down the street. They ran out of the bar to see two men on horseback heading out of town going west. The marshal's horses were both tied up to the hitching rail in front of the jail. They mounted the horses, and stopped when they saw a couple of women yelling for help in front of the café down the street.

Chapter 8

"Marshal—marshal, those two men shot Mister Conroy. My husband's heading down to get the doc. Arlene is holding a rag over the gunshot until he gets here."

Brett knew nothing either of them could do would help, so they took off going west at full gallop. They saw the tracks heading toward the Mexican border. About a half hour later they caught up to the men. Al fired his weapon in the air and yelled at the man to stop. One of the men fired at the marshals, hitting one of the horses and taking Brett to the ground.

Al returned fire bringing both men down. He rode up and ordered the two men to surrender their weapons. Brett's horse had been spooked when the shot grazed it. Brett managed to calm him down before going over and helping Al with the arrest.

"Are you all right, Brett?" Al said. "It looks like you took a tumble."

"My back and knees took the brunt of it, but I think I'll be fine."

The marshals tied the two men to the saddle horns on their horses and took them back to town. They put both men in jail, before Brett went up to see the doc to check on the man who had been wounded.

"Hi, Doc, I came up to check on the man that had been shot," Brett said. "How's he doing?"

"I'm afraid he didn't make it," the doc said. "Why the limp?"

"One of the prisoners shot at my horse and spooked him and I landed on my side. Al took the two guys down, and they're both in jail now. Where was the guy shot?"

"He took it in the back. I guess he was trying to get away from them when they shot him."

"Did you recognize the guy?"

"No, I didn't get a name for him either. He's down at the undertaker's."

Brett returned to the office, walked back to the jail cell holding the two men and sat down outside the cell.

"The man you shot is dead," you better have a good reason for what you did."

"It was self-defense, marshal. I didn't want to do it but, I had to."

"I might have believed you if the guy hadn't been shot in the back. What happened in there?"

The two hung their heads down. They realized this would be a hanging offense. The Marshal walked back out and sat at the desk. Al came in shortly. He sat down across from Brett.

"I just came from the café. Being early morning, there were quite a few customers," Al said. "They said the three men were sitting at a table, an argument started and one of them got up and started running toward the door. One of the men shot him in the back."

"Did anybody hear what they were arguing about?"

"No, but they agreed there was a lot of screaming and yelling."

"Why don't you go out and check on the other deputies, I'll go ahead and get things ready for court tomorrow morning."

A half hour later Brett finished up. Al's wife brought in lunches for the deputies and the prisoners as the café had closed down for the day. After his wife left, Al went back outside on-duty. Brett walked back to have a talk with the prisoners again.

"Can you tell me what the argument was about?"

"We were partners on a ranch up north. He took all the money we had and ran away last month. He didn't think we could find him. We were here in Tucson on business. I spotted him in the café while we went down the boardwalk."

"Why didn't you just ask him for your money back?"

"We did—first he said he didn't know what we were talking about, and then said we couldn't prove anything. I just lost my temper, Marshal."

"The circuit judge will be here tomorrow morning," Brett said. "I suggest you get your stories straight for him."

Brett returned to the outer office. He added the two men's statements to the paperwork. A couple bar fights kept the marshals busy that afternoon. A little later, Josh came in to watch the office for the night. Al and Brett went across the street for a beer before going home.

Thelma came home a little before Brett got there and begin cooking dinner. Brett put his horse in the barn, fed and watered it and went into the house.

"Hi honey, how's Barbara doing?" He said. "I take it she had the baby?"

"Yes, about 2 o'clock this afternoon. She had a boy this time and he's adorable."

"I'll bet John's happy over that," Brett said. "Have they decided on a name for him yet?"

"They're thinking about Christopher, after Barbara's father."

"Yeah, that's a nice name."

Brett went to the washroom outside and got cleaned up while Thelma got a dinner of pork and beans and hot coffee ready for them. After dinner Thelma cleaned up, while Brett went in the other room to get changed. They spent the next hour on the couch mostly discussing the birth. Afterwards the two went in and went to bed.

The next morning Brett came in the office finding John sitting behind the desk.

"Hi, John, I didn't expect to see you here this morning. Thelma told me about the new baby, congratulations."

"I understand you have a court case this morning," John said. "I take it that it has something to do with the two men sitting in the cell."

"Yes, they killed the man in the café across the street. Al and I chased them for about a half hour. One of them shot at us and spooked my horse when the bullet grazed him. Al returned fire and they surrendered. The suspects claimed self-defense but witnesses say the victim was shot in the back."

Al came in shortly, and the Marshal sent him to the stable for a buckboard. John and Brett went back to the jail cell, handcuffed the prisoners and took them out and loaded them on the buckboard.

They took the men to the courtroom where they were both tried and convicted of murder. The judge gave their sentence.

"You've both been charged and convicted of murder. As you both know that is a hanging offense. In armed robbery cases, it makes a little difference who pulls the trigger," the judge said. "However in a case like this, Mister Murray, it does. I sentence you to be hung by the neck until you are dead. Mister Jackson, you are hereby sentenced to 10 years in the Yuma territorial prison—case dismissed."

John and Brett took the two men out to the buckboard. Both men were returned to the jail because the train wouldn't be in until that afternoon. Al returned the buckboard to the stable, while John and Brett took the two men back, putting them in separate cells.

On his way back to the jail, Al heard gunshots in the saloon. As usual, somebody said something that somebody else didn't like. Luckily, the shooter missed the other man, however, took out the mirror behind the bar. Al had the man handcuffed and in custody by the time the marshals from the jail got there. Al led his prisoner across the street and put the man in jail.

"You've got the bartender across the street mad at you, and you're going to have to pay for the mirror," Al said. "What was it all about?"

"Brad said something about my wife, I don't remember what."

The prisoner then passed out on the cot. Al shook his head and walked out to the office. About that time Al's wife, June came in with lunch for the deputies. Jerry brought in two lunches for the prisoners and then went back for a third. He came out into the office.

"I have a feeling that third one may have been a waste of time. I take it he got drunk because he was snoring and I couldn't wake him up. I left it next to his cot. Well, have a good day." He then left the office.

After a few bites, Brett turned to June. "If Barbara ever quits her job serving lunches here, I'll sure put in a recommendation for you. These beans are top drawer."

"Well thank you Brett, June said, looking at Al. "I don't usually get many compliments on my cooking at home."

Al looked at her. "I guess I'll have to go along with Brett on that one. Why don't you ever cook for me that way?"

June looked at her husband "You want to sleep on the coach again tonight?"

The deputies all got a laugh out of that one. After lunch, Brett and John stayed in the office. Al went after the buckboard,

Jack and les went back to their duties. A few minutes later Al got back to the office. Brett was sitting outside in the sun.

"We'll bring the prisoner out, Brett said, and walked into the office."

A couple minutes later John and Brett brought Jackson out to the buckboard and put him in the back. They delivered him to the train station going to Yuma. They returned to the office, where John got the final documents ready for the hanging the next morning.

"John, why don't you go on home?" Brett said. I can handle things here until Warren shows up. Barbara needs you more than I do right now."

"If you don't mind, I'll do that."

John walked down to the stable and picked up his horse. The attendant had fed and watered the animal. When John rode up to the farm he saw Barbara outside holding Christopher. He took the horse into the barn and gave both horses an apple. He blew Barbara a kiss from the pump and got cleaned up. He walked up and sat next to his wife. She handed their newborn to him. She could see the pride in his eyes.

"So, how did the day go?" She said. "How did the guys like my substitute?"

"Well— Brett said, if you ever decide to quit, they should hire June to take your place. She did fine."

"I take it your trial case got taken care of."

"It went pretty much as I expected. One of the men will spend the next ten years in Yuma territorial prison. The man killing his partner in the café is due to be hung tomorrow morning. I don't know how anybody can claim self-defense when they shoot a man in the back."

"I often wonder how much good the gallows really does," Barbara said. "But I guess it does give closure to the families. I know officials realize it's supposed to deter crime, but sometimes I wonder."

"I don't like it either, but there are cases when it really has to be done," John said. "I'm glad Christopher takes after you."

"I don't know about that. He has your eyes, and he always seems to be hungry."

"Speaking of that, I'll fix dinner for us tonight."

"No need, dinners already in the oven. I fixed baked squab, with all the trimmings."

The two got up and went into the house. John went in and sat down on the couch holding his newborn son. Barbara set the table and removed the meal from the oven to let it cool. She took Christopher into the back room to nurse him. Afterward she came back out. John had put dinner on the table. They both sat down and blessed their new child.

After dinner John told Barbara to go sit down in the living room and he'd take care of cleaning things up. Afterward he joined his wife on the couch. Barbara lay back in his lap and he slowly and gently massaged her head. After Barbara nursed Christopher and put him up for the night they got cleaned up and went to bed.

The next morning John quietly got up, letting Barbara sleep. He put on a heavy coat, got a cup of coffee and one of Thelma's homemade rolls before going out and saddling a horse for the trip into town. He walked down to his office from the stable. He went inside and relieved Warren who had to make an arrest at Jake's saloon. The man lay on the cot with a black eye and blood still on his beard.

"What happened to Everett in there?" John said. "I take it he was in a fight."

"Not until he tried to resist arrest," Warren said. "He was drunk and didn't give me much choice."

The Marshal looked at him. "Did he do any damage to the place or anybody else?"

"No, he hasn't really been that much trouble. I figured if he were sober we'd probably let him go this morning," Warren said. "Our other prisoner cried most of the night. I feel sorry for him not having a family here."

"Barbara and I talked about that last night, but we have to consider the victim's family."

Al came in a little later and the three marshals took the man to the gallows behind the jail. Being early in the morning most of the people there to observe were family and friends of the man killed. Some had brought their children as a warning not to go outside the law.

John walked the man up the thirteen steps to a minister who gave him last rites. The hangman asked if he had any last words. With no response, he placed the noose around the condemned man's neck and the hood over his head. With that he pulled the lever opening the floor beneath the man. He kicked for about thirty seconds after being dropped to his death.

John and Brett returned to the office relieving Al and letting him join the three other marshals on duty. Brett went back to the jail and released Everett, warning him not to take his gun in the saloon.

Things stayed pretty quiet the rest of the morning. Brett walked over to the café and told Jerry they wouldn't be needing lunches that day. June had just shown up with lunches for the men when Brett got back. Al sat next to his wife as she served meals to the men. Afterward he walked her out to her buggy, giving her a pleasant goodbye kiss.

Things stayed quiet the rest of the afternoon. Leaving les in charge, John and Brett walked across to the saloon and got a beer.

John left and went to the stable for his horse. The animal had been fed and watered by the stable hand. He got home to see a light in the back bedroom. After giving both horses an Apple, he went to the pump, cleaned up and shaved. He then went into the house and to the back room. Christopher lay in his pen, and Barbara was fast asleep on the bed. He decided against waking her and went to the kitchen to get dinner ready. Fried rabbit and vegetables had cooked on the stove and were ready to be warmed.

Not wanting to wake his wife, John quietly made his way into the living room. He began thinking about the execution that morning. He could understand family and friends, but he could not understand why other townsfolk would want to be witness. He napped while waiting for his wife. She had nursed

Christopher before coming out to the living room, lifted her husband's head and set it on her lap as she sat down.

Barbara looked down at her husband. "Aside from the obvious, how did the rest of your day go?"

"Things stayed pretty quiet this afternoon. Warren brought in Everett Jennings who got drunk and shot Jake's new mirror, which he promised to pay for, but everything else stayed good."

After dinner the two returned to the couch. Ten minutes later Al came riding in.

"John, we had an after-hours bank robbery," Al said." The night guard was tied up and the thieves got away with a lot of cash. It's going to be dark pretty quick and I have a feeling we won't be able to follow them long. Witnesses said they were heading west, one man sitting outside said he heard one of the others say something about Mexico."

John kissed his wife. He followed Al out the door to the stable where he got his horse, saddled it and rode off toward town. The weather turned cold. Getting to the jail, Warren waited for them. The outlaw's tracks were still fresh and would be reasonably easy to follow until dark. After dark it would be Al's expertise that would lead the way.

A couple of hours later the marshals saw a campfire and assumed the outlaws had stopped to rest their horses. John always appreciated that the marshal's horses had more stamina.

The marshals quietly made their way as close to the fire as possible. The three stood out with guns drawn and told the outlaws to toss their guns and put their hands in the air. Two of them did that, the other decided to take a chance. Warren took him down before he could get a shot off. The other two were tied to their saddle horns and Warren's victim thrown over his saddle.

Late that night the marshals rode into town and the dead man on his horse taken to the stable. The undertaker would be called the next morning. The other two were pulled off their horses and put in jail. Their horses were also taken to the stable. The marshal and Brett returned home. John took his horse into the barn and gave him an extra pail of oats and several apples. He also gave an Apple to the other horse.

John went to the pump where he threw water over his face before going into the house. Being dark, he quietly made his way into the bedroom where Barbara slept. He quietly crawled in next to her.

The next morning when John awoke Barbara fixed a breakfast of ham and eggs for him. Not having had much to eat the day before, he appreciated it. After a cup of coffee he kissed his wife goodbye and went into town, stabled his horse and went down to meet Brett in front of the office.

"John, we may have a problem," Brett said. "A customer at the divinity saloon told Al that a friend of Reese was threatening to kill both you and the circuit court judge this morning."

John thought about that for a moment. "Where's Al, we better take this seriously."

"We are, that's why I'm here. I'll start at the courthouse with two deputies and another deputy watching the Divinity."

The marshal went into the office and strapped on his guns. He felt that if this guy were a friend of Reese he wouldn't have any qualms about shooting somebody in the back. John grabbed his rifle and walked out onto the porch.

Brett stopped him. "John, why don't you go back inside and let us handle this?"

"You know I can't sit in that office all day waiting for somebody to break the law."

"This isn't exactly the same thing," Brett said. "If they shoot you, I'll have to take your job."

A couple of men came riding down the street to the jail.

"Marshal, Billy Ray is just coming now."

"Frank, you two stay here and let us use your horses."

John and Brett headed west toward the divinity. They heard the gunshots in the courthouse. The deputy lay on the steps mortally wounded with a bullet to the head. The marshals slowly made their way to the courtroom. They saw Al lying on the floor near the door to the courtroom. John looked through the window in the door and could see no one. He and Brett made their way back to the judge's chamber.

"Brett, you better go back and see to Al, John said. "I'll take care of this guy."

Looking through the door's window, John saw the circuit judge slumped over the desk and the gunman mouthing off about the judge's decision. The man pushed the judge's head back with the butt of his gun. The marshal slowly pushed the door open and yelled at the gunman to drop his weapon.

The man ducked behind the counter, aimed his gun at John and fired, grazing John's shoulder. The marshal returned fire, his bullet going through the counter and hitting the man. The man stood with a gun in his bloody hand taking careful aim at John. John got off the first shot hitting Billy Ray in the chest, killing him instantly.

John went to the judge's desk. The judge bled from his shoulder. John tied his bandanna in a knot and put it over the wound. Les came running into the room.

"Les, you're going to have to hold this tightly until Doc gets here," John said. "I have to go look after Al."

John ran out of the room and into the hallway. Brett stood over Al finishing the bandage covering his chest. About that time the doctor showed up.

"Hi marshal, is that Al I see on the floor?" Alex said, running toward the body. "What happened here?"

"We were given warning this morning at somebody wanted to kill the judge and John," Brett said. "When we got here the deputy lay dead on the front steps, I came over here to see what I could do for Al."

"The judge was wounded below his shoulder," John said. "I put a bandanna on it the help stop the bleeding."

Alex got down on his hands and knees and opened his briefcase and began applying bandages. After giving Al a sedative in case he woke up, the doctor told a couple of deputies to get him down to his office.

He went into the judge's quarters, and up to the bench. The judge lay unconscious in his chair. The doctor pulled the bandanna off and dressed the wound. He called the deputies in to put the judge on the wagon where Al lay. Les drove the buckboard back to the doc's office.

John and Brett remained at the courthouse until a couple ladies could get there to clean things up. They rode back to the office to let Hank know what happened.

"Hi John," Hank said. "Where have you guys been?"

"We just got back from the courthouse," Brett said. "Al's getting patched up at the doctor's office, he has been shot in the chest. You better let our prisoners know it will be a couple days before they go to court."

John put his guns up and went across the street to Jake's. He found the two men that had come down, warned him and let him and Brett borrow their horses. They saw him come in.

"Well Marshal, thank God you're okay," one of the cowboys said. "What about the judge?"

"He had a bad shoulder wound, but the doc says he'll be fine. Al has a chest wound and Alex isn't too sure about him. I'm heading down there now," John said, turning to the bar. "Jake, give these guys anything they want, it's on me."

"You don't have to do that, Marshal. We were glad to help."

"I think I know both of you will enough to know that, but let me do that for you."

John went down to the doctor's office and up the stairs. The judge lay unconscious on the cot. Al lay on the table. The doctor worked feverishly on him. He looked up at John for a minute.

"I don't know, John," the doc said. "Al's lost a lot of blood."

The marshal walked out of the room just as June came in. She wept when she saw John.

"John, how is he?" June said, almost afraid of the answer.

"The doctor is doing everything he can. Al chased the guy into the courtroom and was shot coming down the hall. It's a chest wound, but it looks like it missed the heart. There is a chance it may have grazed the lung, but he doesn't know yet."

"Well, you stay here with him. I'll have Jerry bring lunches the guys. Tell the Doc to let me know as soon as he knows anything."

John walked out of the office and downstairs. He went across the street to let Dennis know he would need lunches for all the deputies and two prisoners. He then returned to the office to fill out the needed paperwork.

About an hour later five deputy marshals came into the office for lunch. Dennis got there shortly afterward and passed them out.

"Do our prisoners eat like this every day, John?" One of the deputies' said.

"I doubt it, I told Dennis he would be competing with Barbara and June today."

After lunch John returned to the doctor's office to check on Al's condition.

"I've done about all I can do for him," the doc said. "The rest is up to him. I told June she may as well go on home, because Al would probably not regain consciousness until sometime tomorrow."

"I see the Judge is still knocked out.

"He'll probably be out of here sometime tomorrow or the day after. Both men are pretty lucky. I think Al will be fine. He has a pretty strong constitution."

John returned to the office. Les had brought in Jacob Harley from the M&M saloon on a drunk and disorderly charge. As they had just buried his wife the week before, les figured the marshal would go easy on him and let him out the next day as soon as he sobered up.

The marshal had about all he could take for one day and left Les in charge. He went to the stable, got his horse, and headed for home. It surprised Barbara to see him home that early.

John washed up at the pump and went inside giving his wife a kiss. He then walked back to see Christopher. It had been a long hard day.

The end.

u.s. copyright # 1-5867096291

www.ingramcontent.com/pod-product-compliance
Lightning Source LLC
Chambersburg PA
CBHW050205230526
45470CB00001B/251